THE FUN LOVIN' CRIMINAL

HUEY MORGAN

THE FUN LOVIN' CRIMINAL

A MEMOIR

QUERCUS

First published in Great Britain in 2025 by Quercus
Part of John Murray Group

I

A CIP catalogue record for this book is available
from the British Library

HB ISBN 978-1-52944-249-6
EBOOK ISBN 978-1-52944-253-3

Typeset in Scala by CC Book Production

Printed and bound in Great Britain by Clays Ltd, Elcograf S.p.A.

Papers used by Quercus are from well-managed forests and other responsible sources.

Quercus
Carmelite House
50 Victoria Embankment
London EC4Y 0DZ

John Murray Group
Part of Hodder & Stoughton Limited
An Hachette UK company

The authorised representative in the EEA is Hachette Ireland,
8 Castlecourt Centre, Dublin 15, D15 XTP3, Ireland (email: info@hbgi.ie)

I would like to dedicate this book to my wife, Rebecca.
My best friend and my partner in crime.

Contents

Contents

THE FUN LOVIN' CRIMINAL

Chapter One

New York

When I got back to New York City from North Carolina, I was still trying to process my separation from the Marines. It had been one wild ride. All the crazy things I experienced while serving still hung heavy on my mind. It felt weird being a civilian – a free man – again. The last time I was afforded this kinda freedom, I fucked around and caught a case. This time needed to be different. I had a good friend who lived downtown and he was my first stop, seabag and all.

Claudius's crib was in Stuyvesant Town, a housing project built after World War Two for the returning veterans. It is a huge 'PJ' that stretches from 14th Street to 23rd, and from the river all the way west to 1st Avenue. Claudius and I had lived there with our moms, respectively, since the late 1970s. Now fast-forward some 15 years, it's 1992, and things were a lot different. But in some strange way, it felt both like home and not like home at the same time.

Claudius buzzed me in. The two of us had been friends since I was about 11 or 12, and it was cool to see him. We hugged, we laughed and, without too much fanfare, proceeded to smoke what was my first joint in a few years. It was everything I had hoped it would be. As Claudius played some tunes, I caught up with all the hood gossip. Turns out lots of our mutual friends had gotten locked up for drugs. Even among those who hadn't, there was a feeling of desperation with the street dudes we knew from back in the day. I knew I wasn't gonna get into that shit again, but what I was gonna end up getting into, that I didn't know. I knew what I'd like to do, but whether that might happen was another thing.

Ever since we were kids, Claudius and I had talked about being involved somehow in music. Like me, Claudius knew he wasn't cut out for the straight life. We were both serious music lovers; the heavier stuff like Sabbath. Metallica had put out an EP with old punk rock covers a few years prior and we vibed to that a lot. I was into the guitar stuff like Zeppelin and the Stones, but Van Halen's crazy guitar wizardry got my attention big time. I listened to their stuff so much I think I got some of my showbiz pizzazz from Diamond Dave by osmosis. When I was 12, my mom had got me my first recording device – a TASCAM Portastudio. Ever since then we had tried to start bands and create music, in the hope of one day making it big. Claudius is a singer and has a prog/ psych rock band called X Ton Gusto, which I had named for him when we were both younger – but I digress like a motherfucker.

Like I said, it had been a while since I had blazed a joint, and Claudius didn't mess around with no shitty weed. When the joint took hold of my mind the stark reality of my situation spun into focus. It was like a figurative page turn, like everything bursting into colour when Dorothy arrived in Oz. I was not in the Marines anymore.

Boom.

'Hey, man,' I asked Claudius, between coughing fits, 'do you know a spot I could get a bunk for a few days while I make a plan?'

Claudius did one of those cute little intakes of breath he always did. 'Sally and her boyfriend have a place with a chick who used to date my guy from the Warzone,' he replied between puffs. 'Down on Ludlow Street. They got a spare room, but it's fucking small, bro.' Cough. 'And there's a lovely view of a shaftway.'

As Claudius passed me the joint, I thought about my former lodging arrangements in the service. A little room on the Lower East Side (LES) didn't seem too shabby in comparison. 'I ain't got nothing else poppin', so I guess I'll give that a shot. You got her number?'

Claudius laughed, shaking his big old head of dreadlocks. 'Yeah, I do. And yeah, you don't.'

Sally was a cool rock singer, tall and zaftig, like a cuter version of Mama Cass. Originally from some podunk broke-ass Southern town, she came to NYC with her high-school sweetheart and a bunch of big dreams. A John Cougar Mellencamp song made flesh.

Sally's crib on Ludlow Street was right by where all the shady drug shit on the Lower East Side went down. Just downstairs from the apartment was Max Fish, the original hipster bar. Junkies from uptown and the West Village would slum it there, trying to cop heroin from the Puerto Ricans on Stanton or crack from the Dominicans over on Rivington.

The apartment itself was a crappy fourth-floor walk-up decorated in a combination of 'modern hippie' mixed with random religious candles from the bodega, and patchouli. There was a shared kitchen and a small dining room area with a banged-up sofa and a small framed photo of Jimi Hendrix on the wall. As for my own room, Claudius wasn't kidding when he said it was small. It was tiny and unfurnished with a view, if you could call it that, of the 'space' between our building and the next one over.

I bagged a futon from a Chinatown shop and a clothes rail from the Salvation Army store. With the addition of a plywood bookcase for my library (all 34 volumes) and a desk lamp for reading, I now considered my new place home. I hadn't had my own space for a while and it felt good to be able to have one again.

Even so, adjusting to civilian life wasn't easy. I didn't sleep much unless I'd been drinking or taking Valium, or both. Most days, I struggled with feelings of depression and anger. But that was ok, I thought. If I was feeling – however dark those feelings were – it meant I was at least alive. Some of my best friends weren't. That gave me the faith I needed in myself to try to get myself better.

I began the process by visiting a shrink at the VA (Veterans Administration). I did my best to take the therapy seriously but when I turned up at the hospital on 23rd Street for my appointments all I saw were these Vietnam era vets, down to a man, fucked up somehow. They were trying to get any help they could, but whether it was physical rehab, the therapy or, finally, the drugs, nothing was working for them. It left these guys empty, destitute and hopeless. I didn't want to end up a victim of the VA and its bureaucracy of ambivalence so I decided one day to never go back.

I was determined not to jump back into the street stuff that got me into trouble in the first place. After about a month I felt that enough time had passed and excuses had been made to my reflection in the mirror to put my own plan into action. I was starting to settle back into civilian life, playing in a band with Sally called Kingstone. Sally was one of the backup singers and I was on guitar. We sucked, but I was playing lead again, in a band!

I was also finding ways to make ends meet. I started off as a bike messenger, but that sucked as much as the band. I ditched my bike one afternoon after almost getting killed by two taxi drivers exacting revenge upon each other with their cabs on Hudson Street. I then got a job at Macy's as a security guard for the Christmas season. That was a crazy job, having to care about shoplifters. It wasn't my bag either, but it didn't involve me dealing with death on a daily basis, and that was cool with me. That part of my life was over. Or at least I thought it was.

One day I came back to the apartment on Ludlow to find Sally's boyfriend going berserk. He was crying when I came in the door and ran up to me like he wanted me to do something. But when I tried to ask what the problem was, he was too scared to tell me.

I instantly clicked back into Marine mode.

Sally's boyfriend started to try to explain, but through the tears and sobs he wasn't making any sense. I knew in my gut it was bad and just hoped it wasn't Sally. She had become a good friend during my stay and I felt protective of her and this boyfriend of hers. I had met kids like these two before and knew they were a little naïve. The boyfriend was so worked up that I assumed Sally had gotten herself the sort of trouble a dumb kid from South Cackalacka can fall into in New York City.

'Hey, man,' I said, trying to calm him down. 'Is Sally ok?'

When he finally came around, catching his breath, he nodded yes. Thank God, I thought. But that was as good as the news got. It was our other roommate, the kid told me. He had found her OD'd in her bedroom. Most people on hearing that would have been as much of a mess as Sally's boyfriend. But with what I had dealt with in the Marines, this didn't bother me as much as it should have.

'Really? She gets high?' I muttered as he led me down the hallway to her room. Despite having lived there a while, I still didn't know this roommate all that well. She was always real cool with me. We would have friendly chats in the kitchen. Her boyfriend was in a band with a former Marine who would hang out at Claudius's house now and then. But I never went into her room. I was never invited and I never asked. They had their own crew and I was an outsider to them.

When we entered the bedroom, it reminded me of something Wednesday Addams might have had if she'd lived on the Lower East Side. The roommate was on the floor, bent over herself. She lay in a position that looked like she had fallen asleep against the side of her bed. Her face was blue and purple in places where her blood had settled.

There was yellow snot and spit around her nose and mouth. It reminded me of the many times I had been around death before: the familiar smells but also always a sort of diminishment of spirit. Death takes what it takes, and what it takes is missed by us all.

I checked her neck for a pulse more in hope than expectation. Nothing. When I looked closer, the stuff around her nose and mouth was like a crust. Even in Marine mode, it made me turn away. I told the kid, more forcefully than intended, to call 911. He was trying to be out in the hallway, away from her body anyway, so this gave him the excuse he wanted. He ran to the phone in the kitchen to call the police. I stayed where I was, trying not to look at her.

When Sally's boyfriend came back some of his colour had returned. He told me the cops were coming, and we both stood there with nothing to say. It was apparent that the kid had never seen a dead body before, and I thought back to how I'd felt seeing my first one. It is different for everyone, but I remember feeling that it was weird to see a person's body without life. Like it was a glitch that would remedy itself and the person would spring back into action. This wasn't gonna happen here, though.

It was bad enough she'd OD'd and that her family would have to deal with all the stuff that goes with having to bury your own kid. But seeing her all crumpled up on the floor made me want to move her into a more dignified position.

I gently told the kid what we were going to do. 'Hey, look at me . . .' I put my hand on his shoulder, like he was a young Marine about to get in his first gunfight. 'It's time we moved her onto her back. She wouldn't want to be found all fucked up like this . . .'

The kid's eyes jolted between me and the dead body scrunched into the side of the bed at our feet. I thought he was going to be sick so I patted him on the back to return him to the moment and went over to the dead girl. 'You hold her like this . . .' As I put my hand on her back, I could feel she was still warm. I tried not to put that information into my voice. 'I'm gonna ease her out of this crouch she's in.' The kid nodded dumbly and got into position, looking at me like I knew something he didn't.

It was all going ok until, as we moved her, she made a groan. That freaked the kid out so much he lost all composure and left the room, fighting back tears. The groan had made me shudder too, but I didn't let on. I'm good at hiding that kind of stuff from the rest of the world. It's called military bearing.

The groan and my reaction brought me back to somewhere, some*one* that I hated: the part of me that becomes this person who cuts all the bullshit and commits and executes. I turned mindless but aware of how cold everything inside me became. Afterwards, I'd be freaking and crying and shaking like Sally's boyfriend. But in the moment when it's me relying on me, it's business.

As the roommate lay on the floor facing the ceiling, I noticed for the first time how pretty she was. She had blue eyes, dark, almost black hair; strong features with a cool rock chick style. It was such a fucking shame that she threw her life away without ever really getting a chance to live it. Did she do this shit to herself on purpose? Or was she dabbling and took too much? Her eyes were open and it was hard to look into them, but I did, looking for something.

I didn't find anything. Death took it.

I put my hand over her eyes. Closed them, saying a silent prayer.

The cops and the EMS guys showed up soon after. They immediately shooed us out of her room to take statements while the paramedics did their thing. The pair of police officers took me and the kid into our respective bedrooms to ask what happened. As I told the officer with me what I knew, it seemed like he was a little pissed off at me. I asked him what his problem was and he motioned to my old dress blue uniform on my coat rack against the wall. With his head he said, 'You shoulda looked out for her.'

'Fuck you.' I stood up from my bed, suddenly seeing red. It was not a good thing for me to get so angry so quickly but that was what I'd been like ever since I'd come back home. The cop could see I was angry enough to lose my temper, so threw some bullshit rap about me potentially catching a case over moving the dead girl to put me in check.

I had sized the cop up when he got to the apartment, like I still do with every man I meet. It's a Marine thing. My job had been to fight and kill other men, and that leaves you with residual side effects. Back then in the nineties, if the need arose, I kind of had a plan to kill any man, if I needed to. This asshole was an overweight mook, like most NYPD downtown in the early nineties. I knew that, if I wanted to, he wouldn't be able to get to his piece before I got him in a rear choke after a hand-strike to his fat face. The cop and I did a little staring contest thing for a minute or so, and then he stood up and broke the spell. 'OK, tough guy, you're good, ease back.'

'Yeah,' I replied as sarcastically as I possibly could. 'OK, officer . . . sir.'

By the time he and his partner reconvened us in the dining room, the EMS guys had bagged up our roommate's body and left. I never saw her again or had a chance to say goodbye. By contrast, the cops gave the distinct impression by their nonchalance and lack of eye contact that they saw stuff like this every fucking day. That they didn't give a fuck anymore, and thought all of us deserved this shit.

After they had gone, I went to my room and started to shake and weep like a kid. I didn't want to spend another night in that tomb, so I packed up my ol' seabag and left the

Lower East Side to the junkies, the cops and the hipsters. I called Claudius to see if he wanted to smoke another joint.

So that's how I ended up on this here stoop on East 26th Street in Manhattan, between 2nd and 3rd Avenues. Claudius had a guitar player friend, Mike, in his band X Ton Gusto. It was Mike who offered me a sofa in his apartment until I could get a roommate situation going somewhere else. Mike's place was in an ok neighbourhood with an immigrant working-class tilt, a few big mental hospitals and three methadone clinics in a five-block area. It was also a few blocks away from the VA, were I went once a week to meet with a well-meaning psychologist to discuss why I was depressed, anxious and self-medicating my way through an undiagnosed stress disorder.

Mike's apartment was a little ground-floor one-bedroom affair, with a rickety raised loft-platform, a kind of split-level living room where his roommate, Aram, slept. Under the rickety loft was an empty, narrow fold-up futon sofa, aka my new 'home sweet home'. Aram was a wild-ass North African artist type. His parents had worked at the United Nations, which is how Claudius knew some of these more wild cats. Claudius is originally from Lesotho and his mom worked for the UN at UNICEF for years. The UN employees all sent their kids to a school called UNIS, the United Nations International School, near East 23rd Street on the East River.

Claudius went to school there and lived in my neighbour-hood growing up, which is how we became friends. His mom travelled the world for her job, which was why Claudius had the crib to himself most of the time.

Back on East 26th it was a hot summer night and I was chilling with these new friends and roommates out front on the stoop. The sounds of the city were easy on my ears after years away. The sirens were a musical crescendo to the neighbourhood's already busy rhythm. It felt like I was back in the centre of the universe. How I missed this place, New York City.

'Hey!' I was pulled out of my daydream by the lady from the apartment facing the street. Leaning out of her open window, she had a pretty blonde page-boy head, which seemed to be tilted at me in particular. 'I'm Angie,' she introduced herself in a huge New York accent. 'You wanna come in for a joint and a blowjob?'

The effect had probably been more potent ten years ago, but Angie had the sort of attitude and sex appeal that most men who got this offer rarely turned it down. Don't get me wrong, I'm not a prude, but when I decide that I'm gonna live somewhere, I don't then make an effort to complicate the situation.

'Hey, Angie, I'm Huey,' I smiled back. 'How you doin', girl? That's a real nice offer there, but if I pass on the fellatio, can I still smoke a joint?'

Angie didn't bat an eye. The lady had composure that I had rarely seen in civilians. Instead, she winked at me and nodded her head towards the door of her place. As I got up, Mike and Aram were making faces and shit, trying not to laugh. 'See y'all in a few,' I smiled. 'If I'm not out in an hour, come get me . . .'

Angie's living room had a good vibe to it: lots of wood, very high ceilings and a loft where somebody like Aram probably slept. The rest of the apartment looked like it might go back to another bedroom and a bathroom I couldn't see. Angie had good taste and style, and the apartment was appointed very well. High windows with translucent curtains framed the evening's street lights. A Nag Champa incense stick made its presence known. Oscar Peterson oozed from a little boombox on the kitchen bar.

I love jazz music, always have. Mainly I love it because I have no idea how to play jazz music. It somehow removes me from the process of trying to figure it out theoretically. It thankfully turns off a part of my ADHD brain and that then allows me to detach cognitively and simply enjoy the sounds for what they are, like most other people do. Oscar Peterson is one of the greats, so I knew this lady had class.

Angie sat down across from me on the floor. Making light of her new position in front of me, she levelled, 'You sure about that blowjob, sweetie?'

I blushed and blurted out, 'I'm kinda particular who I let see my boxers.'

Trying to change the subject, I asked, 'You need a light for that thing?' as Angie pulled a tray from the coffee table. On it were papers and weed and the big rolled joint I'd come round for.

'So what's the story, Huey?'

Angie was more striking than I had first noticed. She must have been about 40 and carried that very well. Dancer body. She had skinny ankles and wrists, a thing my mom always told me to look for in a woman. But it was more in her eyes and manner where who she was shone through. Angie looked directly at you when she spoke, aware of her aura, not caring what you made of it. She was brave in the way she presented herself without caveat. It wasn't bravado, that's different. Bravado leaves the taste of blood in your mouth, like a slap. This wasn't that. I could tell she had at some point proven her bravery to herself and it made her eyes shine just now.

I started to tell Angie my story. She let me draw a picture of a man who did his bit in the Marine Corps and wanted to start a new chapter in his life. As I spoke, she looked at me like she was trying to spot a 'tell', or something. 'I'm just getting reacclimatized to this weird-ass society again,' I explained. 'My plan was to start a band and see what I can do with that.' I decided to keep the nightmares and depression to myself. This was the private stuff that everyone has tucked away. The stuff that no one could ever get close to understanding without thinking you were a raving psychopath. Right? 'I started playing guitar in junior high,' I continued to blab. This weed was *good*: she must give me her connection. 'I got really good, played in some bands, did some gigs at CBGB's.' I was talking more to this stranger than I did to my VA shrink. Was I auditioning, or something?

Turns out, I was. But more on that later.

When I first got out of the service, people I met, mostly women, would ask me if I had killed anyone. It's something every veteran gets asked, but isn't something every vet wants to answer. The few times I got asked, I said that that was my personal business and moved the conversation on. This time, Angie started by telling me her body count first.

'This one son of a bitch tried to pull me into his car and I knew he was a fucking perv, so I tried to shoot the fat fuck in stomach with this little .25 I used to carry when I worked that catering gig, ya know. Hit him in the ankle. I fuckin' ran like hell to the deli by the elevated subway on Ditmars . . .' As Angie waved her finger around like it was loaded gun, I could see she was reliving the story as she told it. She was hyped up from the weed and her face was tight with emotion. When she stood up, she almost fell on me. Her breasts pushed up against me and it kinda sent me wild. It had been a while and she was acting real cute. '. . . Then

I call Beansie.' Angie was standing in front of me, all eye contact now, high and shit, making gestures like she was on the phone. 'He goes and fuckin' tells me to toss the piece in the river on the other side of Astoria Park, so I start to run to the river, but this is the crazy part . . .'

Angie described how she eventually got to the river, threw the .25 into it, the guy lived, 'And that was that.' She finished, wiping her hands clean.

Angie was absolutely hilarious. A true blue New Yorker, it was like listening to a female Goodfella. This lady was a one of a kind: I hadn't had so much fun with a woman with my clothes on, ever! Over the course of the evening we got to know each other better. Angie had a kid, she told me. A teenager named Isabella. She was at her dad's for the night, she said with a knowing wink. She was persistent, I'll give her that. I told her how I was looking for a job and she suggested I got over to the famous Limelight nightclub on 6th Avenue and get a gig as bar staff: 'They're always hiring good-looking kids like you,' she purred. Like a tiger to a lamb.

After a couple more hours' conversation about our mutual love of jazz and Miles Davis's *Kind of Blue* album, I stumbled out of Angie's apartment with my dignity still intact. I have just made a friend, I thought to myself as I walked down the hallway. But while I was right about that, what I didn't know was what else my new friend was about to become.

Chapter Two

The Limelight

My new home on 26th Street, between 2nd and 3rd Avenues, was a neighbourhood lively with low-life, which had a certain calming effect on me. The underside of society, free from the bullshit that the normies seem to love, is something I've always been drawn to. I had never subscribed to the normal way of doing things and now that I was embarking on a quest to become a rock star, or die trying, this seemed like a fitting place to blast off from.

My new hood was a combination of addicts, weirdos and 'leftovers', a strata of New York City that only really existed in Manhattan. Leftovers were those regular folk from when it was possible to live in Manhattan on a working person's salary. As the Yuppies had taken over, so the doormen, electricians and transit workers were heading for the Bronx, Brooklyn and even fucking New Jersey, leaving Manhattan ripe for the gentrification process. The poor people were mostly moved to Section 8 housing, which is a nice way of saying 'projects', on the Lower East Side. The last of the leftovers were just about ready to throw in the towel, a transformation my new hood was in the final stages of going through as the reign of mayor David Dinkins was coming to an end.

Bellevue Hospital was two blocks away on 1st Avenue. Bellevue is world famous for its psychiatric ward, where all the criminally insane people caught by the NYPD were held for observation. From there they would either be sent for trial or be evaluated and released. Every Friday afternoon, there was a clear-out of the padded cells to make space for the coming weekend rush. Around 4.30 p.m. those bumped from the psych ward would make their way west, walking like zombies with their Thorazine shuffles, heading for the subways on Lexington Avenue and on to the hinterland of New York City in search of brains.

Scattered around the side streets between 23rd and 34th were a series of methadone clinics. The way the methadone programme worked back then was that if you were high on dope and got pinched for some crime, you could ask the judge to send you to the programme instead of the city jail on Rikers Island. But like most social programmes in NYC at that time it fell short of the mark it was trying to hit. All those people who had tried to kick one poison to stay outta jail were now nodding out on another one.

It was terrible to witness. I would later write a song about the addiction epidemic I saw there during this time, 'Methadonia': '. . . *they weeble and they wobble/but they don't fall down . . .'* I think it got to me particularly because I felt an affinity with those guys: I knew that I was never too far from joining them myself.

Despite all the urban blight, I felt strangely at home in my new hood. I felt like a guy with a little bit of hope. I still had my issues sleeping. That didn't seem to be going away any time soon. I had abandoned my therapy sessions at the VA because there didn't seem any chance of getting the help I needed there, and wasn't sure where to turn next. But I had met up with a few musician cats and my prospects were looking up.

Angie, too, was becoming a good friend. I would hang at her place and blaze joints when her kid Isabella was at school. She got me a few catering gigs at this private members' club downtown in the financial district right near Wall Street. We worked some of the gigs together, smoking joints on our breaks and laughing at the uptight clientele.

Whenever we talked about how New York City used to be, it wasn't long before a wise-guy story featured. I kinda figured Angie was knee deep in 'the Life' by this time. I didn't pry and did my best to stay out of most of it. By contrast, it always seemed to me that Angie was asking me stuff that didn't really bear any relevance to what we were

21

discussing. Like, she'd ask hypothetical questions that were morality based and then we'd gab on why I said what I said. It was an exercise that always had some 'right' answer and a whole bunch of wrong ones. 'What would you do if your wife was very sick but the doctor was busy? Would you interrupt him and make him see your wife? Or, would you wait like a lamb?' That kind of thing. I would ask her why we were talking about this. She would always say, 'I'm just curious, Huey, sue me.'

I'd laugh and keep the conversation moving, but it always stuck with me.

I got a job at the Limelight nightclub. The Limelight was one of three different clubs I worked that were owned by the same guy, Peter Gatien, who tried to keep his crew honest by moving them between bars. As well as the Limelight on 6th Avenue, Peter ran the Palladium on 14th Street, the Tunnel on 27th and the West Side Highway, and later Club USA in Times Square. One half of a power couple, his girlfriend was the heir to the Benihana fortune. Peter had an eye patch like a pirate and stood outside his clubs watching the door people and security with his one good eye. We would make jokes about it, but if Peter looked at you with his 'crazy eye' you felt uncomfortable, for sure.

On my first day, I was a busboy, picking up cups and litter at the Palladium while George Clinton and P-Funk did their thing for four straight hours. The job might have been mundane but the music was amazing. Listening to these bad cats laying it down I felt like I had woken up from a coma. The lighting show from the concert was transfixing and the music moved me in a very deep way.

Parliament, George and the vibe they created made me so inspired to get my music back on track that I blew off picking up shit and went up to the balcony and smoked a few joints and had a songwriting moment. I wrote most of the lyrics to my song 'Crime and Punishment' that night on a few napkins with a sharpie. I should have given George Clinton a writing credit. No one noticed I had skived off work because the place was so packed, and I did my best to clean up as fast as I could when the lights came on. Everything seemed possible now I was free of the Marines and back home in NYC.

Before long, I moved on from being a busboy to working as a barback, supplying the bartenders at the bars with beer, alcohol, mixers and ice throughout the night. It was better than being a busboy and was a cool-ass job compared to what I was doing in the Marines.

I only got about $2.50 an hour on the books but each bartender I supplied would tip me 20 per cent of the tips they made. Some of the bars had up to ten bartenders and if you knew your stuff there was money to be made. I made friends with an Irish guy, Mackie, who was in charge of all the barbacks, and he gave me some of the best shifts. I could make up to $200 a shift on a busy weekend night if I hustled, and I did.

This was the era of the superclub in NYC. These clubs were huge, with thousands of people wading through those spots every night they were open. They were like mini cities where people would come to be the real version of themselves, the version they hid from the rest of the world. The club was where they could express whatever feelings they had without judgement. It was fascinating to witness this sub-culture up close. I wasn't a club kid but spending most of my time at one rubbed off on me, making me even more tolerant of different lifestyles than I had been.

Each night the clubs played different kinds of music. This was '93–'94. There was a big dance music element, of course; house and techno were staples on the weekends. But during the week, and on Sundays, the clubs would transform into landing zones for very different scenes. On Sundays the Limelight would have a rock and roll night called 'Rock and Roll Church' that would be packed: Ozzy, Guns N' Roses, Pearl Jam and other huge bands would perform. The Tunnel had 'Mecca', the craziest hip-hop party New York City ever gave the world.

I was working at Mecca when I came up with the idea for another song. Before the night got underway, a security guard we all knew as 'Mike' would parade through the club carrying a shotgun with a garbage bag over the barrel in one hand and a large plastic jar filled with 10mg Valiums in the other. Shaking the jar, he would shout to us all, 'Anyone need a Scooby Snack for later?'

The night was so crazy that Mike's gift was more than welcome and I'd always grab a few for later so I could get some sleep. But it would always make me smile thinking how easy it would be to rob the club if Mike wasn't walking around with a shotgun handing out Valiums. So I wrote a song about this robbery fantasy, and eventually it made me a bunch of money.

Mecca wasn't the only helping hand in my musical journey. Tuesday night at the Limelight was the indie night, Communion, and it would be there that a promoter from the UK, Neville Wells, introduced me to two cats who ended up in my new band.

Neville knew I liked to smoke weed. One day before the club opened up he came by the bar as I was setting up and introduced me to this kid with weird bleach blond hair hiding under a wool beanie who called himself 'Fast'. Brian 'Fast' Leiser was the guy who was the driving force in Moses on Acid, a techno/house band who Neville managed. Fast would program the beats and produce most of their music. I'd heard the name before because Neville gifted the band's merch to the club's security guards who were always looking for a black t-shirt without blood on it. He was about five years younger than me and hopelessly naïve but I liked him. He and I hit it off and quickly became friends.

Fast introduced me to all his club-kid mates and the scene that existed around the clubs. Steve was the drummer in Moses on Acid and they all lived in a loft on Park Avenue South. We would all hang out together in the coat-check area of the Limelight, smoking weed and meeting cool people. I met a dude named Mateo there. His main gig was opening up for the headline DJs, and he was really good for someone so young. Mateo and I formed a special relationship. He became like my little brother and I protected him from the weirdos at the clubs looking to take advantage. In fact, I was becoming the big brother for my all-new group of friends. I was older than them and they gravitated to me. It was a good deal. I treated them with the respect that no one else at the clubs did. They took me out to after-hours raves and gave me ecstasy.

It was at these raves I realized, with the help of the drugs and the company I was keeping, that I was beginning to heal from the trauma I had suffered in my life to this point. I could talk to these people about the struggles I was having and they wouldn't judge me. That was really something. Most people judge because thinking is difficult and takes time and effort, but these club kids, the products of all types of bizarre upbringings, were the most understanding and compassionate people I had ever met.

That said, I still didn't get all their music. Techno and hard stuff in that vein made my head ache. I did catch a vibe with some of the more ambient stuff they played at a club called NASA. Junior Vasquez at Sound Factory was a high point in terms of house music and overall atmosphere. But I still preferred the music I loved. Rock and soul music were in my blood and when I heard elements of that in the house stuff, it inspired me to connect the dots between traditional rock and soul to electronic music. That's where Fast and I met up and started really talking about music.

I also got a girlfriend for the first time since I got back. Her name was Belisa and she was a really cute blonde bartender who was paying her way through a doctorate in psychology at NYU. Belisa was so into me that without my knowing it she had started writing her doctoral dissertation on me and, more specifically, my mental health challenges after separating from the Marines. She knew I was having trouble sleeping, how I was drinking way too much and topping it off with a few Valium if I could get some. I had reluctantly opened up to her about my struggles, thinking she would use her expertise to advise me. Which sort of happened, but not in the way I expected. Belisa's teacher at NYU was someone called Dr Joyce Wyden. After reading about me in Belisa's dissertation, she told her, 'I must meet this young man . . .' Through Belisa's unauthorized thesis I ended up finding a life-long friend and therapist.

Joyce was a very kind little lady who could have been in her fifties when we first met, it was hard to tell. She was real short with a cool hippie vibe, and treated me like her long-lost little brother; lots of hugs. I wasn't raised with a lot of affection so it felt good to have that.

Joyce's offices were on West 10th Street and 6th Avenue in Greenwich Village and we met there once a week. She asked me about how I felt about the state of my mental health. It sounds strange but I didn't know I'd had an opinion on it until then. The haphazard therapy I got at the VA was not really about me but more how the VA wanted me to know that they were not responsible for my mental state before, during or after my service. That seemed kinda fucked up to me at the time, which was one of the reasons I never went back. I wanted to change how my head was working but, like most people, I had no idea how to start.

My new shrink was now trying to help me navigate all this mess in my head and prosper as a person in this 'walk-a-day world' as she called it. Joyce gave me the idea that I could create a blueprint of how I wanted my life to be and then build it. The trick, she explained, was to tune into the famous Jon Kabat-Zinn quote, 'You can't stop the waves, but you can learn to surf.'

Joyce explained about how everyone has a burden to carry. It wasn't going to get any lighter but therapy could help me arrange the weight so it wouldn't keep hurting me as much.

That was the single best piece of information Joyce laid on me. It felt comforting to know that everyone had a rucksack they carried with them, inside of which were burdens and problems they could never get rid of. Therapy would help me look into that heavy rucksack of problems and try to rearrange them for when I put it back on. I loved her for that. I was ready to look into that pack, even though I didn't have any clue as to what was inside, and was more than a little scared as to what I might find.

Chapter Three

Philip

My new friends were part of this new black art/rock movement that my man Claudius was down with in NYC at that time, but they were also augmented with a few black veterans. Philip had been in the infantry in the Marines and we hit it off the first time I met him at the nightclub where he worked. It was like being a panda and seeing another panda in the wild. You can't believe it at first, and then it's all sunshine, rainbows and off-colour jokes. We spoke about how things were different back home, how you couldn't act like a feral Marine and not end up in jail. Philip had been back in the civilian world six months longer than me and worked as a security guy at a nightclub called Life. I'd come through and hang out, Philip letting me in for free and hitting me off with a few drink tickets.

Until the night I got into it with a guy out front on Lafayette Street.

It happened when a couple of friends and I were heading outside the club to smoke a joint. Out front, this dude was making a scene with Philip and the other bouncers about trying to come in. He was waving his hands around and yelling about how bad he was. Good luck with that one, Philip, I thought. All I wanted to do was slip by and smoke my joint. But while I was passing the dude and his mini-drama, one of his waving hands hit me on the head.

'Yo . . .' I grunted, instinctively pushing him away from my personal area.

'Yo?' The guy was full of booze and Friday-night frustration. I just want my joint, I thought. But looking me up and down, he decided to take a swing. The dude's punch was aimed at my cheek, but I had more than enough time to step away from his sloppy approach. As his body went into full extension he was sent off balance. I was about to counter when I clocked a shiny piece of something in his waistband.

A small black automatic pistol.

I couldn't let him get to this gun. It didn't matter if I did lay him out; you could never be sure you were gonna knock a grown man out cold with one punch no matter who you are. The odds of a clean knockout were no more than even, which when a gun was involved was not a risk worth taking. I spun my punch back into my chest, pulling it, and stopping my momentum. I shot a side kick instead, dropping his back foot out from under him and grabbing at the gun.

As he fell over deflated, I stood over him, his pistol in my hand. It was a black .25 calibre automatic, looked like a Beretta. Without thinking, I charged the weapon. It made a familiar sound as the slide scraped a round from the magazine into the chamber. *Click-clack.*

'Hey. Easy, Devil . . .'

I turned to see Philip standing behind me. He had his best 'please don't shoot me' look on his face and his hands out by his sides. The other security guys were standing in shock and awe behind his outstretched arms, still processing what maybe took two seconds to go down. The guy I had fucked up was groaning about his leg, but I couldn't really hear because of the pulse pounding in my head. It was a sound like a siren but on a low frequency. A sound I knew only too well: a deep throb I used to hear when I got stressed out in the past. Before long it started to abate, letting me take in my surroundings once more. It wasn't a good sign, but at least I could hear my man Philip speaking to me.

I took the gun down from my ready position, removed the magazine and slid the receiver back again, popping out the unused bullet onto the street – *clank* – making the gun safe. I took my first breath in probably almost a minute, blowing it out of my mouth. 'I'm sorry, bro, I . . .' I was embarrassed as hell.

'Huey, just gimme the jammy and go home.'

I handed him the pistol and magazine, stooped to grab the unspent round.

'It's all good, Devil,' Philip said as I passed him the bullet.

'Devil', or 'Devil Dog', is a nickname United States Marines call each other that comes from World War One. When the US Marines first fought the Germans in France, the Marines conducted themselves with such ferocity the German soldiers reverentially nicknamed them 'Devil Dogs'. Needless to say, it stuck.

'Roger that,' I managed, unable to make eye contact because of my loss of military bearing in front of a brother Marine. That Devil nickname was barely deserved. I welled with shame for snapping and losing my shit in the street like that. The other bouncers were all laughing and telling me I was a bad-ass white boy but Philip knew where I was coming from. As I turned to leave, he caught up with me and slowly put his arm on my shoulder: 'Brother, we all have this savage in us. We are killers, bro, killers. That's what we are deep down. Us Marines ain't supposed to let no chump civilian like that get over on us like that, shit . . .'

I was laughing with him, or at least trying to. I was also trying not to cry, mostly out of relief. Philip was just like me. I was not alone in this madness. What they say is true: Marines are indeed a breed apart. When people call it a cult, sometimes they're right, sometimes they're wrong. 'Shit, he had no idea, did he?' I laughed as we paused at the curb.

We had walked west to Broadway and Philip had his hand up, hailing a taxi. 'No, but I did.' His tone got more serious. 'You might want to think about not coming by here for a few weeks, Huey . . . until things blow over.'

For a moment I was lost in the headlights from the cars barrelling down Broadway towards us. I felt like I might have lost a good friend over my behaviour. 'Bro, I'm so sorry about all this shit . . . I get so mad, so fast, like . . . I can't control the throttle and—'

Philip took my shoulders in his hands and looked me in my eyes. 'I know bro, I know. I have this shitty anger thing too and it sucks. But I have made adjustments in my thinking that have helped me get to a point that I can see the runway. And I can make the fuckin' runway as long as I want . . .' Philip pointed down the long avenue, theatrical as fuck. 'Don't let anyone shorten your runway, bro.' His arm rested on my shoulder again. 'For real, man. It is as simple as you thinking good thoughts, meditation, bro. Med-dee-tay-shun . . .' He spelled it out just like that. 'And stop drowning your sorrows. Them sorrows ain't worth your life or the lives of the guys who didn't make it back, man.'

The traffic light changed. As a fleet of taxis and other cars advanced on us, Philip's hand went back up to hail one of the yellow limousines.

'I don't have taxi kinda money, I take the train,' I said as a taxi slowed to a crawl. Philip was a big black guy and taxi drivers were notorious for not stopping.

'Yeah, I know, but not tonight.' He gave me a 20-dollar bill and a bear hug and sent me on my way back to 26th.

Chapter Four

Joyce

I have always had an affinity for the West Village. When I was a kid my mother enrolled me in an after-school club in the neighbourhood. As a teenager I would hang there with the cool kids on 8th Street at the double-decker pizza joint across the street from Electric Ladyland Studios. I loved the vibe in the area, the arty types who'd lived there in the 1970s had left it less pressurized than where I lived. I loved, too, the brownstone buildings on the side streets, well maintained and harkening back to the turn-of-the-century NYC of Tammany Hall and Teddy Roosevelt. Whenever I visited it always made me nostalgic for the life I had always wanted to live. So when I discovered that Dr Joyce Wyden's offices were on West 10th Street, a leafy block that was one of my favourites in New York, it felt like a good sign.

I was nervous about going. I was a little freaked out about what Dr Wyden would make me do. I didn't really have a grasp on therapy or how it worked and Belisa was not good at explaining it to me. I knew that it would entail me looking at my life in detail and I wasn't sure I could do that success-fully. I had suppressed a lot of my childhood memories and just plain ignored the stuff I had experienced in the Marines. This was the reckoning I wasn't sure I was ready for.

Dr Wyden's building was a smallish four-storey brown-stone, its ornate window boxes brimming with flowers. Inside, the foyer was more stylish than I had anticipated. Small highlights of colour accented and contrasted against the turn-of-the-century artisan ironwork that weaved its way through the design of the building. The feel was modern, the art on the walls tasteful and clearly placed by someone with a good eye for that sort of thing. I wasn't in a museum, but it had the feel of one. The building was probably a co-op where the tenants chipped in to keep it nicely kept. At the end of the hall was an antique elevator, one of those sardine cans where you pull the rickety gate across, press the button and pray. As the elevator reached Joyce's floor, it made an almost terminal sound and clunked to a halt. I pulled the rickety gate back open and pushed the door out onto a dimly lit hallway which had an antique feel. It felt old but new at the same time, the light sconces demurred down to the ground, the walnut brown walls giving it a cosy ambiance.

At the end of the hallway Joyce was waiting for me at her apartment door. She was tiny, barely five foot tall with her longish red hair tied back in a paisley bandana. She wore an oversized cardigan with a blue-and-white Breton shirt underneath, the sort of smile reserved for close friends and wire-framed glasses low on her nose.

'Welcome, Huey.' Her soft voice echoed down the hallway. 'I hope this isn't too much of an inconvenience for you.'

Her smile was so disarming that I tempered my gruff reply as best as I could. 'I was under the impression I didn't really have a choice, ma'am . . .'

As Dr Wyden ushered me in, she placed her hand on my arm. That might not sound a big deal, but it was unusual for me to be touched. It is something I have an issue with most of the time, and I froze instinctively.

'That girl loves you, Huey,' Dr Wyden tapped my arm to ensure she had my attention. 'I think between the two of us we can get you to a place where you'll want to be here.'

Did she mean her office, or had Belisa revealed more about where my head was at? There had been a few times lately where I'd told Belisa how I felt inside. I'd made a crack about the Brooklyn Bridge and how I wouldn't leave a mess if I jumped off, but wasn't sure how much I'd been joking. I'd been down and struggling with a sense of hopelessness, and part of me, I worried, was making the comment to see how the notion of suicide sat with me. I felt stuck in this zone between thinking about dying because I couldn't see any relief to my tormented mental state and wanting to change so I could live a meaningful life. It was a strange place to be in, giving me a perspective unique to people who seemingly have nothing to lose.

I noticed Dr Wyden's smile again. The one that transcended my bad mood and apprehension and made me feel like I wasn't being a burden at all. Maybe she really did want to help me out and I was being silly by worrying. That was something I hadn't considered, someone who just wanted to help me help myself.

Dr Wyden's office was a two-bedroom pre-war apartment where the living room served as a waiting-room area and the offices, which she shared with another professor from NYU, were what would have been the bedrooms. She offered me some water, which I declined, my nerves starting to ratchet back up again. I sat down on the sofa offered while Dr Wyden settled into her seat opposite me. I perched on the edge; she curled her legs underneath herself like a cat, and patted her lap to begin: 'So tell me, where would you like to be in a year?'

When I had first agreed to see Dr Wyden I had thought a lot about what kind of sorcery modern psychology was. I had asked Belisa a bunch of questions as to what I could expect, so I could steel myself for what was to come. But even with all that prep I hadn't expected such an open-ended question. The silence as she waited for my answer only heightened the pressure. I could hear the ticking of her wall clock out in the hallway as I calculated a response. The tick of each second felt like it was bearing down on me.

It seemed like the question hung in the air forever. Joyce just sat there patiently, smiling a neutral smile, letting the synapses rapid-fire through my brain. My mind was racing. I had thought about all of this for long enough to know that it wasn't something I could do alone. At the same time, I hadn't been able to make the leap to ask for anyone's help. It scared me to rely on others because in my experience people had let me down when I had. Belisa, who was trying her best to look out for me, was stepping up and showing me there was another way, and now this nice little lady with her hippie scarf was doing the same thing.

I cleared my throat. I had made a decision. 'I guess,' I finally replied, staring at the floor, 'I would like to be in a place where I can function without all the booze and drugs, but I feel that it is way too big a problem to overcome.' I took a breath. Having struggled to start to speak, it suddenly felt as though I couldn't stop. 'So I then feel depressed at my failure to do so. And then I get anxious about how to get to the heart of the matter, and by that time I'm either already smoking something to numb the anxiety or on my way to getting a drink.' I had become overloaded again and I could tell it was showing. It made me ashamed that I even couldn't control myself in front of Belisa's professor. My head felt hot, my vision narrowed, my pulse throbbed in my temples. I was going down again. Shit.

Out of the corner of my eye, I saw Dr Wyden gently but firmly raise her hand, palm out. As I watched it glide towards a 'stop' position, I paused.

Then Dr Wyden paused.

She met my eye. Or, rather, I met hers. After a few seconds, though it felt like longer, she smiled. It took a moment longer to process what was happening. I was used to the inevitable sense of suffocation under all the stuff I now had to get through, the runaway of feelings for me to ride. But the snowball of emotions that had long plagued me had somehow been stopped before it started. It didn't make sense.

'Did . . . did you just do that?' As I spoke, I realized I was almost on the verge of tears.

Dr Wyden lowered her hand and shook her head. 'You just did that. I merely showed you that along with your play button you also have a pause. Just like on a ghettoblaster.'

While she giggled at her foray into jive talk, her point hit home as though it had been shot into me. Up to then I had had no idea that I could influence how my mind worked. I could control my thoughts? Rather than the other way round? It sounds naïve, but I had concluded this relationship was something immovable. I had to play the cards I was dealt, and that was that. That the relationship could work the other way round was an epiphany for me. 'Wait up, Dr Wyden . . .' I tried to make sense of what I'd just learned.

'Please . . . call me Joyce.'

'Joyce, what kinda magic was that? I've spent a lot of my life not being able to control that sequence, and now with the wave of your hand, I suddenly have a grip? That's crazy?' Another realisation dawned. Not only had the snowballing stopped, but I hadn't gotten all riled up. And rather than pacing back and forth in fury, I was still sitting down on the sofa.

'It's something your subconscious wanted to address first, apparently,' Joyce leaned a little forwards. 'I just let you and your subconscious know that you had the power all along. And the ability to exercise it. That's all.'

I was shocked by this revelation. It was hard to take in. 'The feeling of self-doubt and fear of failure,' I tried to explain. 'They always followed. And since I've left the Marines I can't think straight because of the stress that over-loads my circuits . . .' I had tears in my eyes now, I could feel it. 'But you . . . ok, I' – Joyce smiled at me again – 'just stopped all that from happening.' I put my head in my hands and wept.

Understanding this new perspective left me feeling a little light-headed. I'd never dreamed I could understand why I thought the way I did. But now, for the first time, I had a new, unfamiliar feeling. Hope.

Ever since I can remember I've been sad. Looking back, I've probably struggled with depression throughout my entire life. When my father left my mother and me when I was about seven, there seemed to be a dark cloud over everything that was left behind. One moment I would forget about being abandoned, the next I would be reminded by something around the apartment and brought back to the reality that my father didn't care enough to stick around. Feeling I wasn't good enough and that I wasn't worthy of a father's love was really tough at times. I remember my mother taking me to a psychologist when I was about 12 – it felt like she couldn't even be bothered to understand my feelings; instead she subcontracted what should have been something a parent did naturally to some random asshole. It wasn't what I needed from her. She was struggling too, of course, but it didn't make a difference to a kid who only wanted to have his feelings understood by his mother.

One of the things I can always recall as a kid was not feeling like I thought other people were feeling. There was always a sense of deep dread about not being good enough or not being loveable. I'm sure my father's abandonment has a lot to do with it but I also remember my mother having bouts of darkness that she tried to hide but I saw all the same.

Was the depression hereditary? I don't know, but I sure felt like I was swimming against the current from a very young age. I had moments of hopelessness almost every day growing up. Initially, I thought everyone did. On the days I felt good about myself I would eventually feel guilty for forgetting that I was not supposed to feel good about myself. The only thing that could make me feel like I was worthwhile was my music. It never dawned on me that there could be another way to cope. I'd learned to believe that I had been wired a certain way and this was me fulfilling the programming, right?

Wrong.

'The brain is fully programmable,' Joyce started to explain, once I'd settled down. 'Didn't you learn skills in the Marines that changed the way you thought about how you do other things? That is programming. This mission we will embark on will help you re-program your brain and get to where you want to be.'

At least I knew where that was. I wanted to be in a place where my mind and my soul were working together, rather than the feeling I'd had of late that they really didn't like each other. I was ready for another mission, just like the Captain Willard character in the movie by Francis Ford Coppola, *Apocalypse Now*. I just didn't want to go on a suicide mission, which was where I was worried my headspace was taking me.

'Hey, Joyce,' I continued to press. 'Why is it I can now see I can do something about this head of mine, but just this morning I felt hopeless? Am I like . . . crazy? For real? I mean, sometimes I feel like it's not worth it. I get all these bad thoughts about being a shitty human and that the world would be a better place without me and . . .'

As I was speaking, Joyce had gotten up from her perch on the sofa opposite me and padded over to rest on the arm of my armchair. 'Crazy? No. Crazy people think they're not crazy, it's everyone else who's the nut,' Joyce reassured, patting my back.

As I said, I really hate people touching me. It goes back to my childhood and a very bad experience with a priest. I got beat up for stealing some quarters from the collection box by a priest, and in doing so he went way out of his way to creep me the fuck out. I was about 12 at the time. I was an altar boy and, with another kid, got a job cleaning up the church after-hours. The donations box was stuffed with quarters and so we used to steal a few dollars' worth to play video games at the bodega. It was a nice hustle, until the priest caught me at it, and unleashed his anger. The priest, who was a younger guy at the time, about 30, smacked me around pretty good on my face and on my ass. He pulled my underwear up past my trousers and dragged me around the rectory shouting how he should make me suck his dick. When he was finished with all that, he grabbed my face roughly in his hands and told me I could get fucked for what I had just done. I knew what he meant. That revelation and the weird way he looked at me made me very uncomfortable with being touched by anybody from that point onwards.

Joyce, though, felt motherly in the way she touched me. Like when she touched my arm when I had arrived, it felt warm, caring rather than creepy or salacious. It wasn't something I was used to; it felt foreign and comforting at the same time, all rolled into one.

I found myself doing the laugh/cry thing again, a move I'd lately made famous in my midnight laments. I would walk the streets drunk. I couldn't be like this around my roommates, so I'd head into the New York night and cry and laugh and be a nutcase. I knew no one would notice because this was New York City and that kind of stuff happens every day.

'So when I feel all this all at once, I can stop it?'

Once I'd started getting it back together, Joyce had slipped back to the sofa and was sipping at her tea. 'You just did. You can do it any time you choose from now on, my dear.' Joyce placed her tea cup back down with a chink. 'The truth is, we all have this backpack we carry around with our stuff in it. Baggage.' She laughed and tutted to herself, 'I forget you Marines know about packs. I once had a boyfriend who was a Marine. He told me some stories.' She paused, took a breath, then continued. 'We all have this pack we carry around. When events happen in our lives, we just toss it into the pack to deal with later. But after a while all the stuff needs to be rearranged. Not looking where we are tossing it makes it settle into a position that is hard to carry around every day.'

I sure had a heavy pack on at the moment. It seemed like a lot to ask for Joyce to help me with it, but she was doing her best to make me feel at ease and comfortable with talking about myself, and I got the feeling I was in the right place.

'What we are going to do,' Joyce explained, 'is to look into that pack, and arrange everything so when you put it back on and go out into the world, it won't kill you before you become who you really want to be.'

It took a lot of soul searching, but I realized that I had been able to balance my mental health and my life only because I was being so ignorantly tough about the pain I was going through. That, and obscuring the pain indefinitely with drugs and alcohol. But at least that pain was now something I could identify. I could find the source of where my pain was coming from. With Joyce's help, I could understand which people or events had left me with trauma, and how to process it all. Meeting Joyce made me realize how low I had been. As I started to get it together, the dark thoughts I'd had about killing myself began to slip away. There is an old saying about eating an elephant, and it has to do with small bites. First I had to find the elephant or, specifically, elephants. With Joyce's help, I realized that I might learn where to look.

Chapter Five

Jennifer and Dori

'You did *what?*'

As well as Dr Joyce, who I had started seeing regularly, I had a second therapist in the form of Dr Jennifer. A roommate of my girlfriend Belisa's from college, she was a very well to do and newly minted psychiatrist who had just set up her own private practice, which, according to Belisa, was all thanks to her very wealthy doctor father after a residency in Harlem. Dr Jennifer, who was seeing me *pro bono*, had a plush office on the Upper East and a style that was the polar opposite of Dr Joyce. Personally, I couldn't care less if she was loaded or where she interned. I just wanted to get some help with my mental issues, and this help was free. However, this overlap with therapists was starting to get complicated with their different approaches. Dr Jennifer had immediately put me on drugs; Joyce was trying to get me clear of all that. It came to a head when I decided to ditch the medication Dr Jennifer had prescribed for me.

Celexa is a drug that is used to fight severe depression. I'd started taking it when Dr Jennifer and I started my treatment about four months previous. The drug makes you feel less depressed by using an inhibitor that prevents your brain from regulating chemicals like serotonin. Serotonin and other similar compounds are a big part of mood swings in your brain's cocktail of chemicals, and making them unavailable is supposed to help depression.

The drug is called an SSRI (selective serotonin re-uptake inhibitor), and when you first take it you have to wait a month or so for it to kick in and 'even you out'. I took the drug for a month and waited it out, and then I started feeling weirdly numb. Numb to feelings that, yeah, fucked me up – but also numb to good feelings as well. The result was that I had been having trouble locking into my musical headspace: it's hard to write and play when you can't feel anything. That was the big catalyst for me beginning to think this drug was not for me, much to Dr Jennifer's dismay.

'I just stopped taking it . . . so what?'

Dr Jennifer looked like she was gonna cry.

'Is that so bad?' I asked. I thought that she would be happy, but she was anything but.

'You could have died . . .' Dr Jennifer was getting all

worked up and started to grill me with questions. 'Did you have any suicidal thoughts?'

I sighed. 'Not anymore than usual, doc.'

'What does that mean?' she asked. Another question from her spleen.

'It means that I didn't kill myself, despite all the opportunities that presented themselves while I was on the "jones" from this evil shit you gave me.'

I was trying to make a joke out of the situation, which is what Marines do when serious stuff gets brought up. But Dr Jennifer didn't like my sense of humour and, I suspected, she wasn't too fond of me as a person either. I can tell when people don't understand me: that's kind of standard, it happens every day. But Dr Jennifer was one of those younger academics who didn't understand the need for warriors in our shared society. I think she thought everything would work itself out if these testosterone filled gorillas (people like me) would quit smashing up our nice stuff when they 'got the PTSD'.

When I told her a few of my more intense stories, she looked at me like I was from Mars. She even called Belisa to warn her I was on the edge. I decided not to bring up the collection hook-up gig that came from that whole mob thing. I thought I could be mostly honest but, like Oscar Wilde said, you had better make them laugh while you're telling them the truth, or they'll kill you. I'm paraphrasing, of course.

The longer the sessions went on, the more I got the feeling that Dr Jennifer thought I was beyond help; that whatever mental illness was plaguing my mind was eventually going to win. That is a shitty way to be made to feel by your mental health professional, even if she was giving you her time for free. Despite my opinion of her opinion of me, I continued through the sessions as best as I could; there was other shit at stake.

'Huey, do you feel like things are better now that you've stopped taking the Celexa?'

The honest answer was: 'No, not really.' I still had overwhelming thoughts that I couldn't completely control. But having begun to see Dr Joyce (who had radically different ideas about my therapy) I felt I was getting more from her approach than the drugs that Dr Jennifer had immediately put me on.

'I had a few rough days, but they passed,' I tried to explain. 'I can feel stuff again. Before, I was kind of dead inside, you know? I think that's way worse than feeling all the bad stuff. You can see all of it happening . . . but it's like it's on TV, removed from your control . . .' I knew I was shrugging her concern off, but that was because I felt she was more interested in her professional reputation at this moment than me. Her questions felt like she was running down her checklist for 'duty of care', or so it seemed to me.

But I didn't want to piss Dr Jennifer off too much, because

while I wasn't a fan of the Celexa she had given me, she also prescribed me Valium for the times that I needed a 'chill pill', and Ambien, a heavy-duty sleeping pill that makes you trip out bad if you drink on it. I knew that because I drank on all these pills, and I tripped out plenty. I didn't want to disrupt the supply chain, so I chilled her out with some lyrics. 'If this medication wasn't working, Jennifer, you would have weaned me off it, right?'

Dr Jennifer nodded tightly, arms crossed. She was still mad at me so I kept cooking.

'I just accelerated the process.' I held up my hands in acquiescence, 'I know, dangerously so . . .'

Dr Jennifer looked like a teacher whose dumb-ass student finally gets the point. Her arms unfolded and rested in her lap, neutral.

'. . . So, yeah,' I made a face. 'I'm feeling better . . . like I made it through the fog.'

Fog was an apt description. Celexa was like a fog where everything was translucent and vaguely obscured, my feelings hung in a limbo of clear jelly. I was now free of that horrible purgatory where everything was, no ups, no downs, just 'whatever'. Having gone cold turkey, my crazy brain was now mine again; at my request this time. Whatever weird shit I was thinking and trauma that was messing me up, I now knew at least it was authentically me and not the result of some substandard chemical alchemy.

'Huey, you've got to be honest with me from now on.' Dr Jennifer was giving me the 'what for' now, so I sat quietly and took it. 'How can I accurately help you if you continue to undermine my treatment?'

'Yeah, sorry ...' I muttered, thinking of my Valium supply and how fucked up it would be to have to find another connection, not to mention the Ambien. That stuff was gold dust.

'I think,' Dr Jennifer concluded, 'moving forwards you should make a list of the drugs that you take and when you take them.' Dr Jennifer was only two or three years older than me and this was her first sortie into private patients. I knew I was making it really difficult for her, but I was becoming more and more disillusioned with the Jungian approach to psychotherapy. Valium and Ambien or no Valium or Ambien, this homework assignment was fucking ridiculous in my opinion.

I stood up. 'Jennifer, I'm not going to make any list.' I concluded things for myself now. 'I think that I would be better served with someone else as my doctor.'

I wasn't trying to make a big scene but I wasn't getting better under her care and I realized maybe she wasn't the right person, after all. That was my justification in being so blunt.

Dr Jennifer didn't want me to get off so easy. 'What are you going to do now?' She sneered as I made for the door, like it was a challenge, or something. I realized after a beat that she meant as far as my mental health journey went. I stopped and told her with both barrels, so to speak, from the doorframe. 'I'm not going to shove all those fucking pills down my throat in the hope that one of them will make the nightmares stop.'

Jennifer was looking uncomfortable at my reaction and I quickly quelled her fears. 'I'm not going to lose my temper with you, sorry. I'm just tired of feeling like whenever I say something bordering on ... well,' I made the crazy hand gesture (index finger circling my temple) to ease the tension. She laughed in relief and I felt bad for making her feel scared in the first place. I should have known better than to show my temper.

I continued, speaking more calmly now. 'Jennifer, you seem like you can't imagine anyone saying the kind of stuff I tell you here every week, and it makes me feel like I may be really losing it.' I leaned against the wall by the door and exhaled. It was hard to express this stuff in any circumstance and knowing it was falling on deaf ears didn't make it easier. 'I know that I'm not right in the head.' I held up my palm to keep her from interrupting. 'But that's ok, I'm a work in progress and I'm cool with that,' I smiled. 'It's just that the drugs didn't work and they made me realize things inside me got a lot worse while I was on 'em.' I pushed myself off the wall by the door and smiled a goodbye to Dr Jennifer.

She smiled back, and there was a nice moment there between us, maybe our first.

I could see she was about to say something but I wasn't interested. Before she could speak, I pulled the door closed and took the stairs to the street two at a time. I couldn't work out if I was on the verge of tears or laughter. Was I going crazy or was I going sane? I wasn't sure. It wasn't until I was walking into Central Park, lighting a roach I had stashed in my cigarettes, that another question came to me: why was I so fucking happy after throwing away the best legal drug connection I ever had?

A few months after I had moved onto 26th Street in early 1993, one of Claudius's friends from back in the day had moved into my building. His name was Dori and we became fast friends.

Dori had known Claudius from UNIS and was now back in New York City after spending time in Africa, Israel and the IDF. Dori's family were white Jews from Kenya, and the African part of his trip was to his family home. As he told it, that was all good vibes and amazing stories of wildlife and cool traditional things he learned while growing up there. The apartment he had on the top floor he decorated in an African style, where we'd hang out from time to time and blaze.

The IDF, or Israel Defense Forces, is pretty much the Israeli army. Anyone who wants to be an Israeli citizen in good standing has to serve in the army for at least six months to a year, or have a really good excuse as to why they can't. Like most young people in Israel, Dori didn't have a good excuse.

Anyone who has served their country in uniform understands a few things that most 'civilians' don't. One is actual liberty. When you're in the military there is no 'me time': you are the actual property of your government, and if you don't do what they order you to do, you go to jail or, as we called it in the Marines, 'the brig'.

The other is the sense of responsibility you inherit. You understand that the life you now lead takes place instead of others' who made the ultimate sacrifice for their country. This sobering notion is what makes us most different. It is like having to be a better version of yourself, not just for your sake but for all of your brothers and sisters who didn't get the chance to live out their dreams and aspirations. You're continuing to live your life for you, but in addition you're now living for them as well.

These sentiments were what brought Dori and me together. They created a place where I could talk with someone who had seen similar circumstances and endured similar nightmares. From these sessions we created a solid bond, one that got cemented further in a way I wasn't expecting.

*

One evening I was out on the stoop of my building. It had been a particularly bad week mental health wise. I had been getting very little sleep and that, combined with my new therapy with Joyce, had made me a little frazzled. All the thinking that goes with that kind of stuff had left my nerves raw. And now, to top it off, it was raining and I couldn't even light my joint.

It was an early spring rain, the kind that smells of the warm season to come but is still cold enough to be a pain in the ass. As I huddled into the doorway looking up at the sky, hoping for a ten-minute respite, I saw Dori and his umbrella turn onto the block from 2nd Avenue. He had a very happy walk, which irritated me from time to time, and especially today. But as Dori got closer to the building, he saw me and smiled.

'PFC Morgan!' He gave me this nickname after seeing my boot camp dress blues on my clothes rail. It had my rank sewn on it from when I graduated from Parris Island, one of the two recruit depots of the United States Marines. I kept it as a reminder of how little I was at boot camp.

'My man D! What's up, brother?' By now I had given up smoking the joint on the stoop and was toying with my keys to get in from the rain.

Dori walked up the stoop's stairs and we gave each other a pound.

'Man, I'm done working and I wanna chill and . . .'

Dori looked at me closer than before and seemed to recognize something. 'Are you ok, *mamano*?' That was an African word he used for people that were his friends.

I gave him a look and tilted my hand from side to side.

'Yeah. I know the feeling.'

By now I had unlocked the door and we were at the foot of the stairs.

'Come on,' Dori pointed upwards. 'Let's go to my crib spot and smoke-a the joint, take-a Valium, and listen to Talk Talk.'

I laughed a little at Dori's way of speaking because he made a thing out of his Israeli accent and how funny it sounded saying normal New York stuff like that. But I was mainly laughing about us trying to chill out and get some needed perspective while listening to an eighties band not known for their soothing tones.

As we got to his floor, Dori turned and put up his hands in surrender: 'I know it sounds funny but this album will have you rethink how you think about Talk Talk.'

Rethink? Did I ever really think of Talk Talk in the first place?

Dori, though, was in full flow. 'They recorded *Spirit of Eden* in the dark. Well, most of it,' he explained. 'It came out in '88 after they made millions off their *Colour of Spring* album. I know what you're thinking because I thought the same thing the first time I was told of this amazing record. But, bro, it has changed the way I feel about music.'

That was quite the claim. To be honest, I was more excited about the joint and the Valium than the album. As we got settled in his living room Dori handed me a blue 10mg Valium and a glass of water. I sloshed the pill down and finally lit the joint. Bliss. 'I have to admit that I do kinda like Talk Talk,' I agreed. 'But are you sure it's the vibe we're going for here, my brother?'

Dori was standing over his component stereo pulling a CD from its rack and holding it up. 'Here we go, my friend. Let's get the cypher going and I'll press "play".' He dimmed the lights and made a face like I shouldn't take this as a come-on. He was always playing around making dumb jokes like that.

As the joint got going and the smoke made its way to my brain and changed my consciousness a little, the music faded in like a movie score. I looked over at Dori and nodded. This was cool music. I couldn't tell you what kind it was, other than it made me feel like I had both time to enjoy it and time to reflect about how the sounds moved me. Talk Talk made *Spirit of Eden* in between two of their biggest albums and you can tell it wasn't a commercial endeavor. It was an experiment, maybe one of the last great musical experiments of the twentieth century.

It was spectacular. I was only on the second song when the

combination of drugs and music created an event horizon. In this soundscape, composed almost in the dark in a studio in London, just like Dori had said, I heard the ghosts of my past and the angels of my future. I was bathing in a universe of hope and melody that made me want to live in this augmented reality forever.

In this clearly recognizable instrumentation I heard the possibilities of where I could take my music. I loved the way the production played with your attention by fading sounds in and out of the mix while at the same time making you fill in the gaps of the broken melody in your head. It was true art, remarkable in the sense that you the listener had to shoulder the burden of 'getting it', becoming an active participant in the process of listening to the music. It rewarded me with the feeling of hearing what music could be, as opposed to the current commercial state of the world of popular music. The lyrics, too, had an undercurrent that was deeply spiritual without being pious, letting their wisdom linger in your mental periphery until they naturally hatched in time with the music. It was as perfect an album, for what it was, that I had ever heard.

Don't get me wrong, I don't make music like this at all, but it was inspiring beyond belief. I realized how weaving a certain instrument's lines with another's into an almost seamless phrase could create and relieve tension. I learned how a single lyric can convey much more if obscured ever so slightly in the mix. I heard how this band took the tools of modern popular music and articulated them in a way that was indeed unique. I felt encouraged to make my music as experimental as I could going forward.

Even more significantly, I was somehow able to centre myself in the moment. Like the time Joyce showed me how to pause the sequence of my stress attacks, I could now find a serene place in my mind to meditate for the first time.

When we were about 20 minutes into the CD, the combination of Valium and Talk Talk gave me a sense of well-being that I had not experienced before. I know this sounds corny, but this is what I always knew music could do for me. I could sooth my inner savage enough to allow the other parts of me to find a toehold in my conscious mind. The meditational effect I got from the experience was transcendental. I tried to tell Dori about it but was struggling to find the words. 'My man, this album . . .'

He turned to me from his chair. 'Yeah, *mamano*, it's amazing!'

The album ended after about 45 minutes. I had experienced myriad emotions but one sat on top of the others: a sense of hope.

Hope is the most expensive of feelings in my experience, as it borrows from all the others to make space in your heart. But I now had hope that I could get my head right and make connections with people through my music. It was a good feeling discovering this and would power me forwards immeasurably. This was a waypoint in my journey to become who I was going to be, and I knew it.

Dori was also impressed with my rapid transformation. 'Huey, you love the Talk Talk now, look at you, bro! It makes you think of how things could be different if you can only imagine them that way. Yes?'

'Yes D, you're right. I went into a sort of trance and felt a lot of reconciliation inside of me.'

He smiled like a proud teacher with an eager student. 'It has worked for me too. I'm happy the Talk Talk made you feel good now.'

I still had a whole bunch of stuff to work through but music once again had been there for me when I needed it. Listening to *Spirit of Eden* was one way I found a process to practise what I now know as meditation. I could get so into the music that my mind could quiet itself and begin to roam around and process things that it didn't have a chance to during my walk-a-day life. I was now able to get stoned, listen to music and meditate about my new mission, which was to get my mind to a point that I didn't think it was plotting against my success. I sometimes felt I talked badly to myself about myself: you are your own worst enemy, right? But once I began to meditate and see the root causes of my behaviour as they related to how I dealt with my therapy, I realized that some of the lesser angels of my nature were just trying to protect me from myself.

All along my subconscious was trying its best, like a dyslexic kid pretending to read by guessing the next word, to protect me from dangers it knew I couldn't deal with. This was a big deal to figure out on my mental health journey I was now on.

I was now actively breaking off some time every day to check-in with all the different parts of my mind that made me who I was, and meditation was getting everyone in there to start playing from the same sheet of music. I know it sounds crazy, but there are a bunch of variables that make up me, and now I was getting to know them one at a time.

I met with Joyce once a week and from there on out I also made a 45-minute appointment every week with *Spirit of Eden*.

Chapter Six

The Making of the FLC

When I was a kid just figuring out that my father didn't give a fuck, I was given music by the gods to soothe my soul. It may sound a cliché, but that's what it did. Music also helped me make connections with other kids like me. Kids who were marginalized by a system that valued procedure over outcome. Kids who were smart but didn't want to suck on the status quo as much as the obedient fucks we resented seemed to do.

There was a record store on 2nd Avenue just south of St Mark's next to the Gem Spa called Free Being Records when I was growing up. These guys were a small operation but had big vision. They stocked all my favourites in all the genres: Miles Davis's *Kind of Blue*, for example, was an early addition to my record collection. The main guy, who may have owned the joint, was really cool with us when we'd all clamour in on a Saturday looking to spend our ill-gotten allowances.

There was a rehearsal studio I used to jam at with my friends on 4th Street and we would walk uptown on the way home and browse the store. When we would ask about a certain song that was playing, or an album that was in the window, this older dude would give us a detailed breakdown like it was a book report, or something. He became our guru to the extent that he would suggest stuff for us to check out. I remember he told me that this band from Hammersmith (wherever the fuck that was), The Clash, had a debut record worth checking out. After that epic recommendation I returned to discover albums by Nick Lowe and Dave Edmunds (they joined forces to form the band Rockpile), XTC, Echo & the Bunnymen, and lots of other new acts that were breaking from all over the world. The record store guy was well versed in classic rock too. I got down with Southern rock bands like Blackfoot, Marshall Tucker, .38 Special and eventually Lynyrd Skynyrd.

The Allman Brothers Band and the Grateful Dead were on the radio all the time in New York City and that's how I practised my guitar. I'd put on the radio and play along until there was a commercial, then I'd change to the next station along the FM dial. It was a great way to stay abreast of new styles: rock and soul was all over, but there were also jazz shows and a few small stations playing new stuff from the UK, so I learned how to play a lot of random music.

The soul stuff that moved me most was Earth, Wind &

Fire. They had amazing musicianship where every cat was a killer, but on top of world-class production that founder Maurice White handled, they had incredible songs. The very first 12-inch I bought was Earth, Wind & Fire, *Greatest Hits Vol. 1*. The one with all the King Tut art on the cover. The opening song on that album was a Beatles cover. They did a version of, 'Got to Get You into My Life' (which, incidentally, is about Paul's appreciation of marijuana) for the remake of *Sgt. Pepper's Lonely Hearts Club Band* that the Bee Gees starred in. Terrible movie, but, damn!, what a song.

I listened to punk when it was turning into hardcore, and New York City bands like Cro-Mags were a huge part of my informed opinion on that kind of stuff. The magic of Bad Brains is still unmatched when it comes to live energy, and the cool-kid stuff like The Clash and Elvis Costello cut through because of the great songs. The way I saw it, I could take what I liked musically and leave the rest. I knew what I liked and I had a strong sense of confidence in that taste. I took the swagger and the humanist messaging from early punk and mixed it with the ghetto tough-guy shit the hip-hop scene was going with and made it my own, kinda.

As a teenager, I looked like a Beastie Boy reject walking through my hood with a guitar gig-bag on my back and a boombox in my hands bumping loud salsa. All my friends would laugh at my apparent confusion. I played all the metal stuff on guitar thanks to my two Albanian metal-head homies, Mike and Zeb Leka. Those crazy brothers taught me sweep picking, a crazy technique where you hammer on notes on your guitar without picking them, sounding like you're floating over the notes very quickly. They also encouraged me greatly when I set myself the challenge of learning *Van Halen*'s guitar solo 'Eruption' from the band's eponymous album. (I once freaked Mike Schnapp out late one night at the studio by giving him a rendition of that unannounced. 'I had no fucking idea you were so amazing on guitar!' Mike beamed like a proud brother.)

In those teenage years, I spent five solid years playing guitar every day after school until my mom came home and made me eat dinner. I would then go back and play until she shut me down for the night. Even then, I was trying to make it a career. I figured I could become a studio session guy if I learned as many styles as I could. I just had to be really good at a whole bunch of techniques, which was fine with me because of my very eclectic taste. Music was what replaced God in my life. As crazy as that sounds, I was an altar boy and when I figured God was busy, I got busy with music.

My life was a bunch of sad streets but if I had the radio on I thought the streets were a little less shitty. When I got to a point on guitar where I could feel something inside and then make that come out of the strings, it was game on. All the loneliness that I felt, all the isolation was challenged. I had given myself an epiphany, if you will. The moments I remember as a kid, playing music on my off-brand walkman, hiding between my curtains and the open window of my bedroom. Bumping whatever I could have recorded in my weekly 'pause-tape' cassette mix. I found some of the feelings that I loved in other people's music would creep into my own, informing me on life, giving me a perspective that I hadn't had and a gift that I could keep in my heart. I'm super corny when it comes to music – its sentimentality is never lost on a romantic, and I got all that from music. I have a certain taste in everything from art to interiors, fashion and spirituality, all from my love of music. I spent most days experimenting with my multitrack recorder: listening back to how the tape would degenerate and seeing how that effect was used in other music was how I figured out – shit – everything. My practice on guitar was an obsession that dovetailed into me hanging around the rehearsal studio my friends and I would practise at. The guy there also owned a studio on Broadway and Houston that had some more advanced recording equipment. After a year's worth of Saturdays this cat asked me if I would like to do a session for him on a song he was trying to produce.

Holy shit! A real studio! Oh my lord, I told my mom that I would be out of touch for a few hours – before cell phones things were scary for kids – and to not call the cops.

When I got to the studio with my purple iridescent

Charvel Super-Strat on my back I was almost busting out of my skin. The elevator ride to the top floor seemed to take an hour. When I got into the control room it was the first time I'd ever been in a real studio. The mixing desk was huge and the rows of faders and thousands of knobs looked like something otherworldly; I was amazed and astounded, but most of all I was speechless. The cat who'd invited me over came up and introduced me to the only other guy there. He looked like Shaggy from *Scooby-Doo*, long hair and a stoney smile with sleepy eyes. He gave me a pound like he was 'down' and we sat down and talked about the song.

Shaggy was the drummer and my dude played bass guitar. My man's name escapes me but he was a fly eighties black guy who kinda looked like a downtown Ray Parker Jr (the *Ghostbusters* guy).

The song was a rock thing in a funny time in one part, and we talked that through as well as I could. I hadn't ever had to play anything up to that point, live, in a time signature that wasn't 4/4.

If you're not a musician and this is sounding like maths, I'm sorry. If you're at your first guitar session and you're 15, and the time signature is a learning moment, it adds to the pressure of the moment.

I set up my stuff in the live room where a Fender Twin amplifier was mic'd up across the room from the also mic'd-up drum kit.

Shaggy was hanging out by my amp and we were talking about the pedals I had brought with me. 'Bro,' he began. 'That MXR distortion plus is pretty rowdy, you gonna use that on this?' he asked expectantly.

That was cool, I knew my gig was based on how I played around the studio, but we always thought the older cats were 'weak' when it came to heavy guitars.

'I hope to, but I've, er, got a Tube Screamer here that will chuck up the chords without all the fuzz.'

Shaggy nodded along and when my guy came back into the room and over to his bass rig, Shaggy made his feelings known. 'Youngblood over here,' he thumbed in my direction. 'He's got a little something going on upstairs too, huh?'

My face flushed and I ducked my head back into the gear and got a few sounds up. The amp was nice and it had reverb, which I didn't use for now, I wanted to make this rhythm-guitar track stand on its own if it was my only shot – to muddy it up would be a mistake. When I was close to being ready I asked, all cool like, if it was cool to light a cigarette. I was feeling myself and thought I was in Steely Dan, or something.

'No,' my man deadpanned.

'Yeah, Youngblood,' Shaggy echoed, 'that makes the place smell.'

I was brought back to reality very gently, but firmly.

'You shouldn't be smoking, Huey.' My man was about 35 and had an uncle vibe.

'I know, I'm sorry, just trying to be cool . . .' I made a few sounds on my Charvel to cover my embarrassment.

'Huey' – I looked up and my guy had his bass on and was smiling over to me – 'You're cool enough without trying to be cool.'

'Yeah,' Shaggy said, from the drums. *Boom-boom-boom.* He hit the kick drum, testing it for the engineer in the control room. 'How many other 15-year-olds you know doing sessions?'

I felt a bunch of feelings and they were all good. This was a first time for me in a whole lot of ways. Firstly, I was doing what I'd always wanted to do: in a studio playing guitar! Secondly, these cats, who were bad in their own right, were letting me know I was of value. Being of value is everyone's hope: helping your family and friends, being socially responsible, however you would like to frame it, I was feeling it for the first time. It felt great inside me, and I tried to calm down enough to try to remember the fucked-up time on this song. 'Thanks, guys, I'm real happy you called me and, well . . . shit.'

'Yeah, Huey, you good?' My man had opened the volume knob on his Fender Jazz bass and it started to hum like a car.

'Yeah, good to go . . .' I pulled up my own volume knob on my purple guitar and touched the strings with my right hand to make sure it was on, while fretting the fifth fret with a bar chord. It was in the key of A.

As we started to play, Shaggy made a false start and made a face, 'Damn, trick intro, boys, sorry. My bad.'

We tried again and this time we got through it all the way to the end. There was an outro part that got really heavy and I messed up and didn't hit my Tube Screamer at the right moment. The guys kept playing and nodded at me to catch up. Catch up? What? I missed the cue, why should I?

That's where I learned another valuable lesson. It's multi-tracked, baby! If I fuck up, we can just punch my guitar into the mix another time. But, for now, they knew that I could still keep the vibe up and make their takes 'keepers'. Even if you aren't the keeper this time around, tape etiquette dictates that you try to save what you can.

I caught up and the Tube Screamer did its thing and we all had a bunch of smiles as Shaggy hit the final cymbal crash to end the song.

'Cool!' I shouted, elated.

'Yeah, Huey! Shaggy was sitting up on the edge of his drum seat, 'One more time!'

We all straightened up and adjusted our headphones. When we heard the engineer over the talkback say 'rolling' Shaggy counted us in, 'One, two . . . one, two three . . .'

We all had 'keepers' this time and, as we patted each other's backs on the way into the control room, I caught myself taking a mental snapshot. Me in a studio, playing guitar really fucking well, and now going into the mixing room to hear it all on huge speakers!

Say cheese, Huey!

When I started making music with Fast it was like the beginning of a romance. I mean that in the sense I shared, or maybe over-shared, all my musical inspirations with him. Music for me has always been about making connections. Here I was, so desperate to find that shared bond that I threw caution to the wind and took a leap. I described my musical influences and then some.

This kind of blathering about music and how and what I was inspired by, made my friendship with Fast quite poignant. I became the guy who turned him on to Led Zeppelin. Sure, he'd heard them before but I played him *Physical Graffiti* over a dozen times, giving intense production notes between every track.

I think the reason the first Fun Lovin' Criminals album is so guitar influenced was because of this dynamic. Fast is a genius when it comes to creating new melodies with old samples, but, up to that point, his musical vocabulary was limited to his own tastes. Then I rolled up with some Van Halen and Led Zep, talking shit about how we can take a Joe Walsh riff and rap over it, and it blew his mind. This new well of music I was giving him served as food for thought.

Within minutes of hearing a song I was playing him, Fast would go into his mind (you could actually see him turn off part of his brain), dissect the notes and rearrange them in a new way. This was how my theme song 'Fun Lovin' Criminal' came about.

After a few months of hanging around Fast and Steve's apartment making music they just asked me if I wanted to move in permanently. I had been spending all my free time there with Fast, making music and watching his LaserDisc collection. There was a vacant space in the loft which was fine for me. I had run my course with Fast and my other roommate Pepe. We were already living together on 19th and Park Avenue South and I had been digging around in my CDs for something cool to sample. I picked out Van Halen's third album, *Women and Children First*, and made a face. 'Bro,' I burped. 'This one is a gem.' I showed Fast the cover; the green-and-black artwork and black-and-white photo made it look cheap. Yet the record was almost as good as *Fair Warning*, the band's next album, chronologically. It had some really stripped-back Eddie Van Halen guitar work that lent itself, in my humble opinion, to being isolated by Ted Templeman's production and then sampled.

We had just finished cleaning our coffee table and were settling down to smoke some bong hits and watch a film on Fast's new LaserDisc player. Fast really loved movies. So did I, but he really, really did. We would watch at least two movies a day when we were making music. The LaserDisc player would run a silent movie for us and our composing sessions. It was such a great way to keep a sense of scope when we wrote together. If the movie we had on was a blockbuster, we would challenge ourselves to write a stadium anthem to make it even.

Fast paused over his *Blade Runner* LaserDisc and took the CD from my outstretched hand. 'This David Lee Roth guy is a fuckin' clown,' he laughed.

I laughed back. We all know David Lee Roth is a fucking clown, but I think Fast meant it in a bad way. 'This album showcases a more intimate side of the band.' I had lit a joint and passed it over to Fast. 'The guitar stuff is great,' I continued, doing an air-guitar thing. 'The acoustic stuff Eddie plays on this record is so gritty and raw.'

Fast was laughing at my exuberance and took this as a sign to chop my onions a little: 'Huey, you have got to get with some more recent stuff.'

Fast had a tendency to see me as an older guy who needed a younger guide. I didn't think I needed some kid from the suburbs telling me what was cool, so ignored that comment: 'Fast, you see how all these rap producers like Just Blaze and them, they're taking old soul and R&B hits from the eighties and shit?'

Fast sat back to enjoy my soliloquy and retorted, 'Yeah?'

I rolled my eyes at the ceiling and went on. 'Well, these

rock albums could act as the same type of raw material for us as the other old soul stuff was to Puffy and those other glitzy motherfuckers.'

That made Fast pause and think. I could almost see him began dissecting sounds in his head. I waited patiently.

'Ok . . .' he started to say, very slowly, like it was dawning on him in real time. By this point, I had gotten up and was by the stereo and TV looking to put the Van Halen CD on. '. . . Bro, gimme a few tunes and then we'll go with Deckard over to Tyrell and fuck shit up, ok?'

I pressed play on the stereo. I played a few songs from the middle of *Women and Children First*, like 'Fools' and 'Take Your Whiskey Home'.

Fast was enthralled. 'Bro, rewind that last one . . .'

Van Halen was getting his mind working. In my experience that wasn't something you had either practical physical control over or steering. Your creativity had a mind of its own and you had best keep up and take notes. 'Yeah?' I played the song again and then I heard what he was running in the background in his subconscious. 'That part,' I made a chopping motion with my hand.

Fast nodded. 'Exactly . . .' He was thinking inside his mind again and I waited. 'There's another part but it's on another song and it might not be in the same key . . . but I think it is in the same key.'

'Man, do you have perfect pitch or some such shit?'

I asked, annoyed at this possible development. There are few traits in a musician that are as insufferable as perfect pitch. It makes the rest of us mortals who aren't blessed by the 440Hz gods very insecure, especially stringed instrument players like me.

'Hell no, bro, they're annoying as fuck, right?'

I was nodding along with my homie. 'Word . . .' I countered.

'Anyway, lemme think some more while we watch this shit right here.' Fast held out the LaserDisc of *Blade Runner* for me to take.

'Sure.' I put the movie on and we blazed a doobie watching our man Harry smoke some skin jobs.

About an hour into the film, just about the time where you start thinking that Deckard might just be a replicant, Fast stood up. He walked over to the stereo system next to the TV. He grabbed the Van Halen CD from where I left it and headed into his room, closing the door behind him.

Here we were alone watching a dope movie and my boy gets up like he's possessed and scoops up my CD and dips into his room.

Weird.

Weird, though, was a good way to describe my man Fast. He's kind of nerdy in his manner and his adoration of *Star Wars*. He also had trouble talking to girls and a thing for hand-bells from back when he was a kid, so this kind of behaviour wasn't so bad, considering.

I continued to watch the film in a high definition that I hadn't experienced before outside of a cinema. Ridley smashed this one and by the time Rutger makes his big speech, Fast had resurfaced.

'Bro, come in here . . .' He had left his room door open and was walking back through it. Fast's room was kind of off limits. We were never invited in, and I never pressed, so this was a sign that he had something significant to show me.

The room was not that messy, but it was huge. The loft we all lived in had close to 20-foot ceilings and was white-washed. By the foot of the bed Fast had set up his Ensoniq EPS keyboard on a stand. This seemingly harmless keyboard was really a sampler and a sequencer. It could take a sample, or a sound, manipulate it in myriad ways and then position the sound in a sequence like a four-bar beat that loops. It was really an impressive piece of gear, but it was never used as well as how Fast used it. This cat pointed to the foot of his bed, and I sat down.

As Fast started to tell me what he had done, he abruptly stopped talking. He shook himself like he had a shiver, handed the headphones to me from around his neck and hit a button on the EPS.

Holy shit!

Fast had put together a two-part loop, the first sequence

he played me was the chorus; it sounded like that country guitar was from Van Halen. I couldn't tell where he took the guitar but it worked great. It was bopping to something I couldn't place, and I put up my hand when it played. Despite Fast not having headphones on, he knew what I was talking about.

'That's Gary Wright, "Dream Weaver".' He smiled, knowing that my seventies and eighties CDs were getting a look. 'It's the part when the bass player hits the pop in the second chorus.'

He was proud of what he'd done. Shit, so was I. 'I isolated it before the vocals came back in,' Fast exaplained, 'threw a filter on the bitch, and bam!'

It was great. It was just what I had needed to hear to know this would be my theme song. This would be 'The Fun Lovin' Criminal', in all its glory.

I took off my cans and felt myself getting all emotional. 'Fast . . . what the fuck, bro!' I leapt up off the end of his bed and gave him an embrace. 'This is the shit, son!' I was amped as hell and wanted him to know he'd hit gold with this riff.

'Wait. There's more,' Fast said when I'd calmed down.

'More! What?'

Fast laughed and picked up the headphones off of his bed. Putting them on, he hit some buttons on the EPS. After nodding to himself a few times he then held out the cans for me to take. 'Verse . . . 8 or 16?' Fast asked as I put on the headphones. He meant how many bars long did I want the verses.

I answered, '16.'

'Bet.' Fast hit a few more buttons on the keyboard and the music started.

The drums were a loop he'd put together in a hasty manner but the beats weren't skinny. The bass was that 'all-low-end' dub-type stuff that only hinted at the attack of the note. The riff that made me bug out, though, was the guitar. It was a straight Van Halen sample, but different somehow. I recognized the tone more than the riff and said so. Fast had changed the order of the notes and somehow given it a different swing. 'Yeah, I changed that shit up,' Fast was speaking loud enough for me to hear him over the music in my headphones. 'Don't want those LA law motherfuckers coming around sniffin' after my ass.'

'Bro, how the fuck did you do that in . . .' I looked at my G-Shock, 'An hour?' I shook my head in bewilderment and pointed at the EPS for Fast to stop the sequenced loop playing.

'I was inspired . . .' he responded, self-satisfaction in his voice.

'Well, now so am I.' I stood up and went looking for a pad and some paper.

I returned to find Fast at his EPS keyboard tweaking some

stuff. He looked up and said, 'I got you all set. Just hit this button to start the sequence and this one to start the next one. Remember, verse is that button . . .'

He was pointing to all these fucking buttons on the keyboard but, frankly, I wasn't paying attention to any of that. I was trying to find a lyrical way to start this song, and then it hit me like a ton of bricks . . . '*One, two, three, and I come with the redneck style. Cause you know I'm getting paid by the mile, like Avis I pave this, Fast, save this . . .*'

He hit save on the EPS and then realized it was part of my rhyme. 'Shit, Huey, that's good . . .'

Fast was the guy who put all this dope music together in under an hour and he was now telling me I'm good. He was humble, I gave him that. I laughed. 'Fast . . . man, we are on to something here . . .'

And we were.

The Fun Lovin' Criminal finally had his theme song.

Chapter Seven

Sugar

The head tech dude at the Tunnel nightclub was a friend of mine named Spike. A smallish guy with a tight crew cut and tattoos that were original in their design, Spike lived just over the bridge in Greenpoint, Brooklyn. We had been friends for a while and we would hang out in his office at the ass end of the tunnel that made up the nightclub when he was working. I was the head barback at the time, walking the club during the night to see how the bars were doing and if any of my fellow barbacks needed additional help.

It was on one of those forays that I managed to get myself high as a kite in Spike's office. We had just burned a fat one and I was feeling fuzzy in a good way. Spike had popped a beer from a bus tray filled with ice and bottles and was offering me one.

'No thanks, Spikey,' I held my hands up in surrender. 'I still have to count tips and shit like that.'

He gave me a nod and sipped his brew. 'That reminds me. My dog had a bunch of puppies and I was wondering if you knew anyone responsible enough to maybe adopt one ... or two.' Spike looked fed up all of a sudden. 'Shit, I've got six fuckin' puppies smellin' the fuck outta my crib, bro.'

I wasn't surprised. 'Six puppies is a lot of work, my man,' I said as I was getting up from a recliner in the corner to do my rounds.

As I made for the door, Spike made his pitch. 'Huey, baby. You seem like a guy who loves animals; shit, you are basically one yourself.'

Spike made a lot of jokes like this at my expense because he had an uncle who was a Marine and he knew all about us from stories he'd heard as a kid. I laughed it off, but it was true. I do love animals. So I decided to do a drive-by of sorts.

'Are you home tomorrow afternoon?' I asked. Even as I said it I was thinking, what am I doing? There was no rhyme or reason for me to get a dog. I lived in an alcove in a loft apartment with three other guys. And a cat.

Spike, though, was jubilant. 'Yes, Huey, I am.' He made to hug me and, caught off guard because I was having an internal debate with myself, I allowed his clumsy embrace.

'I'll be in your hood tomorrow running some errands with Mateo,' I said, all uncomfortable from the hug. Mateo was someone everyone knew from being the guy always standing with me when I was outside of the clubs. He had what the kids call 'aura'.

Spike kept on nodding in agreement, elated that I might be going to grab a puppy, or possibly two.

'I'll give you a call,' I looked at my G-shock. 'After lunch, ok?' It had just hit 3.45 in the morning and I still had a few hours of work in front of me. The bars closed at four, after which I had to oversee the clean-up, count and divide all the cash tips from the bartenders. Then I'd pay my guys, the barbacks and busboys, punch out and go home.

'They're really nice puppies, half-pit bull and half-supermutt.' Spike was giving me the hard sell as I headed back to work. 'The mom is a Rottweiler mixed with a lab, they're all super sweet, bro . . .' By now, I'd opened the office door and the club's music was blaring again. So I couldn't hear what he said next, but he was smiling while he said it.

The next day, after I'd done a few errands for Angie, Mateo and I had stopped for a very nice lunch at Bamonte's in Greenpoint, I called Spike on my Motorola flip phone. From the speed he answered, I knew I hadn't woken him up, which was good. Us night workers could be trouble to wake up. I told him we were nearby and asked if it was a good time to see the puppies. From his enthusiastic reply, Spike's eagerness for me to come over hadn't dimmed overnight.

As we neared Spike's crib Mateo got a page from Kevin

the Kid. Kevin was Mateo's de facto little brother, as I was Mateo's de facto big brother. Remember, friends are the family you choose.

Kevin was a line cook working his way up the shitty New Jersey Italian restaurant ladder at a job Mateo had secured for him. I couldn't make out all of what they were saying on the phone and, frankly, despite myself, I was getting excited to see the puppies. But the gist was that Mateo had to go to this restaurant in Jersey and straighten somebody out. So, rather than hanging about, Mateo dropped me outside Spike's apartment building and bid me farewell. 'That was a good lunch, should last me to dinner,' he said as he was driving off.

I took a look round. There were dudes hanging by a bodega directly across the street from Spike's place, who had clocked me and Mateo as we drove up. I reckoned they thought we were likely new customers, but now Mateo left they weren't so sure who I was. I thought it best to get off their scopes so I just hit some random buzzers on the intercom on the apartment block and hoped for the best.

No one answered.

I went to the payphone on the corner and called Spike's house again, but he wasn't answering that either. After that I waited a full five uncomfortable minutes, looking around without really looking around, if you know what I mean. I know the timing because I lit a cigarette and had just tossed it to the curb when I heard the speaker by the door squeak.

'Hello?'

'Yeah, man,' I said, relieved. '*Soy yo.*'

The buzzer kicked the door ajar and I pushed through. Spike's crib was on the ground floor in the back and he popped his head out when I came closer down the hallway.

'Hey, bro.' Spike was keeping the door sort of closed against his head, making sure the puppies didn't escape, was my excited guess. When I got to the door he opened it like he was Walt Disney: 'the magical world of puppies' or some such nonsense. Spike had a flair for the dramatic.

I was met with a waft of dog smell. And then a bunch of little feet slipping and sliding to come and greet me. The puppies were scampering to the door through his kitchen, all uncoordinated and falling about. I immediately sat on the kitchen floor and held my arms out to greet them. They seemed really young but Spike reassured me they were just eight weeks old. The puppies were more like pit bulls than not, most were a dark brindle in their markings, a couple with black-and-white splotches like old time dogs from the movies. There were about seven of them and they were very cute and playful. I lapped them up.

After a while messing around with them, I noticed a brindle puppy who was smaller than the others, having a go at two of her bigger siblings. She was making that growl sound puppies make, like a power drill on low battery. When she clocked me staring she turned her ire my way. Her eyes narrowed and the pitch of her little growl notched up a tone. The puppies were so small that this tiny one fitted snugly in the palm of my hand. I picked her up and brought her closer for inspection.

She had these big brown eyes. Shit, I love puppies. While I was staring adoringly, she leapt from my hand and with her teeth, grabbed my goatee and tried to tear it off. The puppy was so tiny, it didn't hurt or anything like that, but in her mind she was attacking some kind of Goliath. The dog had chutzpah.

Spike and his girl, who I hadn't said hello to up to this point (she's grumpy), were watching me play around with the puppies on the floor, laughing from time to time at my dumb behaviour. 'Huey,' Spike said, 'I think that one likes you.'

I thought so as well.

'Yeah, she's cute and tough, good combo.' As I said this, the puppy made another attempt at attacking me with her surprisingly sharp little teeth. She was adorable. As well as her big brown eyes, her brindle coat had a bunch of tight tiger stripes. I laughed and kissed the puppy's snout, eliciting another growl/whine.

Spike's girl, who I'd just said hello to because I'm polite, told Spike and I to 'have fun' and left the kitchen, walking back into the apartment. I couldn't see through the multi-coloured hippie beads that hung in the doorway but I heard another door close.

Spike turned to me and said, 'Bro, I got no idea what I did to piss her off this time, but she's pissed.' He got up to follow her. 'Jesus, man, I'm gonna see what the fuck is up.'

He passed through the beads, which made the sound of raindrops falling. Then he was gone, into the apartment and out of sight, leaving me alone with the puppies. I looked down into my arms at the unbelievably cute puppy pseudo-attacking my goatee. Then I looked up to the gently swaying beads to see if anyone was coming back. I waited a few seconds. There were some muted voices making it out to me, but after a few moments more, there was no sound or movement. I stood up with the little furry terror still my hands. It was time to make a decision about what to do about this puppy. I took a deep breath, counted to ten slowly . . . and then stuck the puppy in the goose down jacket I was wearing. I zipped it up and left Spike's apartment without a word.

When I had gotten back to my apartment, the one I shared with Fast, Steve and another Goth guy named Jon, I was met by Fast at the door. 'Yo, lemme see this dog, bro!' He was looking past me into the hallway, not noticing the dog's head sticking out of the collar of my bright blue goose down parka. When he finally did, he exclaimed, 'It's cuter than I had imagined! Yo!'

Fast loved dogs and really missed his golden retriever, Blake, who lived with his parents out in the suburbs. He talked about that dog like it was a human member of his family.

'Yeah, she's really sweet and mellow,' I said.

I was making the pitch to keep her to Fast. It was his apartment, after all: his dad paid all the bills, so Fast was ultimately the last word as to whether the puppy could stay. Even though I hadn't thought any of this through, with Fast's love of dogs I figured it was looking pretty good.

At this point, maybe because I had opened my coat, I noticed my chest was damp. The puppy, unbeknown to me, had had a little accident while in transit from Brooklyn. I had taken the G train back to the city and, in all the excitement, didn't take notice of her pee-pee. As I took off my coat, the little puppy leapt into Fast's hands and started to mess around. Fast's face said it all. He looked up from playing with the little dog, and said to my relief, 'It'll be good to have a dog in the crew,'

I smiled back. 'Yeah it will, bro, thanks.'

'It's cool, man.' Fast knew that I hadn't planned on taking this puppy and he was being a good sport about it, for sure, but he did relay a message from Spike, laughing: 'Bro, Spike called and said you can't bring her back.'

I nodded while taking off my piss-damp shirt. 'I figured, but it was like I had to . . . like it was preordained. I didn't know that until we met.'

Fast nodded at that. 'Yeah, dogs are furry angels that choose us.' He paused then gave the puppy another cuddle. 'What's her name?'

It was like I had known it all along. 'Her name is Sugar.'

Chapter Eight

The Sauce

We were driving in Mateo's white VW Jetta with my dog Sugar, barrel-assing it down the Jersey Turnpike at just under a hundred miles an hour. Fast and Sugar were in the back eating Doritos, and Mateo was lighting his cigarette off the butt of his last one. It had been a rough weekend at the club and now, it being Monday, our day off, we were all pretty wiped out and running on fumes. Our destination was Mateo's mom's house in New Jersey. We were going there to record a song Fast and I had just written. Mateo's mom was out of town visiting relatives in Florida, so Mateo suggested we abscond to New Jersey and cut the track out there on the portable ADAT.

Things had got a bit complicated with our normal recording arrangement at Steve's apartment. Steve and his longtime girlfriend Danielle lived together on 22nd Street just off 1st Avenue, and shared their two-bedroom apartment with Steve's brother's studio. Steve's older brother had a wife and a growing family, but was also a musician who wanted a place of his own to put all his amazing studio gear. The upshot was that Steve rented the nice two-bedroom on the East Side and his brother paid half the rent. All Steve had to do was to let his brother use the room during the day.

This was where it all came to a head. We had started using the studio when Steve's brother wasn't, recording our demo for free with his blessings. It was cool for a while but now that we were taking the band very seriously and actively working towards getting a demo together and getting gigs, and ultimately shopping it all to labels, we were at Steve and Danielle's crib way too much, which Danielle wasn't cool about.

'She is sick of looking at us,' Fast had vented one afternoon, 'all fuckin' high, walking down the hallway at two in the mornin'. The chick is from the outskirts of the boondocks . . . and look at you, bro.'

He looked at me. Enough said.

'Shit, even me . . .' he sighed to himself, defeated. 'We're just too ghetto . . . and we scare her.'

Danielle tripped on Steve. Then Steve tripped on us and told us to chill for a week or two and not stop by the studio. Hence the excursion to New Jersey.

*

I had just finished a lyric that was inspired by James Joyce, the Irish writer known for long sentences. That's not the form this particular Joycean inspiration had come from, however. The idea of life, as he put it, being 'the grave and the constant . . .' was something that had stuck with me ever since I first read it in *The Portrait of the Artist as a Young Man*. It led me to thinking how that turn of phrase could apply to my journey so far. Joyce's idea of what might unite us, in this case terror and grief, was my jump-off point. I wrote of my idealism as a new Marine and how after the proverbial veil had been lifted from my eyes, I was burdened with the things I'd done in the name of my country. From one to another, as the saying went, I told of my path from troubled youth, to Marine, to whatever the fuck I was now. That was why I wrote the song to begin with, to answer for myself one particular question. Who the fuck was I?

What every songwriter tries to do is connect with the communal ideas that unite us all. As I took the cigarette butt from Mateo and lit my own Camel from its cherry, I decided to try to 'arrest' the mind in my prose on this new song. My ethos as a lyricist was to not take myself too seriously; fat birds don't fly, and all that. But I did take what I wrote about seriously because the connections my music might make with folks needed to be authentic in its execution. We can all see the fake shit.

The music part of the song was a cool sample Fast had

found, to which we had added guitar and keys to fill out the sound some more. A loop from some hip-hop song was dropped on top of that. Now we just had to record the vocals.

Mateo's mind was never far from food. He had stopped at the Italian grocery store by our apartment in downtown Brooklyn and picked up some things to make a nice home-made Bolognese sauce for our dinner before we left. As we turned off at his exit he grabbed a few mini-cannoli from the bag and gave me one. 'I got some stuff to make a sauce while you record the track.' Mateo was always a team player as well as the chef. 'A nice Bolognese with some linguine and garlic bread . . . Just the thing.'

When we got to Mateo's mom's house Fast and I unloaded our gear into the kitchen and began to set it all up. Mateo, meanwhile, started the sauce. Fast was plugging in the Ensoniq EPS keyboard to the ADAT. As I wasn't going to be any help there, I went to see if I could help Mateo with the cooking.

'Huey, do you want to learn how to make an authentic Bolognese sauce from scratch? Nah?' Mateo was tying his apron on, which read, 'Kiss the Chef' on the front with some lips painted on for comedy content.

'Yeah,' I replied and caught the new apron Mateo threw from a drawer at the counter by the stove.

'Ok . . . first, you gotta get the meat browned.' Mateo slid the ground sirloin in the already hot pan with a satisfying sizzle. 'The trick is when you put the olive oil in you drop in some basil stems, all diced tiny.' He held up his fingers like an Italian chef. 'It makes a nice smell and it infuses the basil into the oil and then the meat.'

I took in the herby aromas as Mateo folded the meat around. 'See here,' he made a small clearing in the middle of the pan, 'there's still some water from the beef that needs to evaporate. We cook it until the water is gone and all that's left is the olive oil. Then the onions.' Mateo had pre-chopped the two small onions, which he tossed into the pan. 'I showed you how to dice an onion, right?'

'Yeah, you did,' I replied, paying close attention. The smells were starting to make me hungry.

'So now we let that cook for a little while . . .' Mateo began rooting through his grocery bag, looking for something, so I asked Fast how things were going.

'I'm almost ready to get crackin' . . .' He held up an affirmative thumb.

'Me too,' Mateo chimed in. We looked back to him, and he said, 'What?' Mateo knew who Mateo was, and he was in the middle of a cooking lesson. Fast would just have to wait. 'Now we add the tomato paste and after that . . .' he continued, smiling to us both, 'the wine . . .'

As Mateo cooked, so, to speak, did Fast. He set up the track on the ADAT and pulled up the sequences from the keyboard, which he'd laid out on the dining room table. 'Ready to go, Huey? You wanna test the mic?'

Fast held out the Sure 57 microphone to me. I took it and looked for a place at the table to get comfy and perform. The dining room didn't have a door, which meant that the kitchen where Mateo was working his magic was two feet away from where Fast had set our stuff up. When I was starting to mic-check Mateo had to take the sauce off the stove because the sound of the simmering was getting picked up by the recording equipment.

'This is a good time to reiterate that you can use either white wine,' Mateo said, holding up a bottle of white as he took the pan off the heat, 'or red. Mom only had white, so . . . it is what it is.'

Everything was in good shape. The sauce was coming together and the song was almost finished. If I could lay down a lead vocal track and maybe a double to fatten up the sound, Fast and Mateo could do the background vocals and we could be back in the city by midnight.

I laid down a really tight guide vocal for us to work from. Once that was recorded, we listened back while Mateo finished up his cooking lesson.

'Now we put the garlic in, it won't burn in the sauce.' Mateo had put the sauce back on the heat, crunching a few cloves in the saucepan and putting the lid back on. 'I got these very nice San Marzano tomatoes from that spot by you in Brooklyn.' Mateo added the tomatoes to the pan and used a wooden spoon to break them up. He was seasoning with salt and pepper when Fast noticed something on my vocal track.

'Bro, this sounds weird.' Fast stopped the digital recorder and played it again. We all listened intently.

'There's some vibration that hits that frequency the guitar is on . . .' I noticed. 'That's feeding back that low tone.'

'What would do that?' Mateo sounded concerned. It was his mom's house, after all.

Fast rubbed his chin. 'Were you holding the mic too close to the top, bro?'

I looked at my hand and how I'd been holding the mic. It wasn't anywhere near a place that would interfere with its nominal operation. I shook my head and lit a cigarette, setting the mic on the dining table.

Fast stared at the microphone on the table for a few seconds. Then he said, 'Do we have a mic stand?' to no one in particular.

We were not in possession of a mic stand, and he damn well knew it. Mateo's mom was a music teacher, so I figured there was an outside chance she'd have one laying around. At this point, Mateo chimed in. 'She's got a few saxophone stands in the garage, B,' he offered, though showed no signs of moving. He was too concerned with the cooking. 'Can I get back to the sauce?' Mateo asked Fast, who was the de facto engineer.

'Yeah, I gotta think . . .' He fussed around with the equipment while Mateo caught my eye. I went back in the kitchen to help him.

'So now the tomatoes are in . . .' he said quietly, glancing around like he was telling me a secret. 'We get the basil, but don't chop it: tear it into little bits.' This was my cue. I tore the basil leaves into the saucepan and Mateo nodded in approval. 'Make sure you stir from the bottom, so it don't stick . . .' He made a stirring motion with his hand.

I was laughing along with him when Fast broke the culinary spell. 'I know, we can use something else . . .' He was looking around the kitchen for an alternative stand, eventually stopping in front of me as I took a sip of my Snapple ice tea. 'Aw shit!' Fast exclaimed. 'We use that!'

'What?' I asked him.

'The Snapple bottle. Look . . .' Fast was pointing to the neck of the bottle which was wide enough to fit the microphone's end into. I could see what he was getting at. It just might stabilize the mic long enough for me to record the vocal track.

'Genius!' I exclaimed this time, proud of my boy's IQ.

We gathered around Fast as he squeezed the microphone into the Snapple bottle. Turned out it was a perfect solution, and it didn't fall over either.

As we got set to track the vocal, Mateo took the sauce off the heat again.

'Before you guys start, I'm putting in one can of tomato puree . . .' He winked at Fast and continued, 'Then I gotta incorporate that, 30 seconds tops.'

Fast made a face like it was all too much to bear, but it was starting to smell amazing with Mateo's sauce in there so it was hard to complain too much. I was always in support of letting Mateo cook food. He was great at it and we got to eat all his great meals. If you didn't get too high, you might learn something. And that day I learned how to make a Bolognese and stabilize a microphone with a Snapple ice tea.

Chapter Nine

The First Gig

'So how was it?' Joyce asked with something resembling bated breath.

Only a few months ago I was a wreck, falling over myself trying to get my mind right. Right enough to start this band and begin to be the lead vocalist and guitarist in Fun Lovin' Criminals, my band. I made time to see Joyce but I also made time to practise guitar every day. I'd had to ask our roommate, Jon the Goth, to borrow his guitar as I didn't own my own at that point. The discipline I learned in the Marines I tried to apply to my dream of making music my life. I would listen to new music every day and try to apply lessons from that experience, the sonics, the subject matter the tempo or feel, to my own stuff.

My own stuff was now looking like a hybrid of rock and hip-hop. Not like how it had been tried before; my style, as I called it, applied the versatility of Steely Dan musicianship with the raw aggressiveness of Eric B. & Rakim's early stuff. The formula wasn't complete but I had an idea of what I wanted to feel when I heard it, and that was a start. My new band were trying to feel it as well, and because they trusted me with my vision, which wasn't fully formed, I had a chance to let my feelings guide the sound. This was the part of the journey I thought was the most important; the beginning. And now I was sat there, telling Joyce about our first gig.

She was really proud that I'd gotten things to this point with the band. So was I, to tell the truth. To get this far was a huge milestone in my musical journey. And I was profoundly psyched to tell her all about it. I didn't really have anyone else that I wanted to share this with that wasn't directly involved. So while I kind of played it all off, my enthusiasm betrayed my cool exterior.

'It was . . . aw shit, Joyce! It was amazing.' I lost my composure and Joyce giggled. Seeing me this buoyant was a welcome relief for her. I'm sure my smiling face let her know it went well, but I went into it anyway. 'I mean, it wasn't perfect – what is? But, damn, we did great . . . I did ok keeping things interesting with the crowd, but yeah . . . it was very cool.'

The first gig of any band should be remembered even if the band isn't. I've had a few first gigs with a few bands, and this one was pretty epic by any standard.

The gig was the very hyped-up birthday party of a very popular club kid named Andra. Andra was good friends with, and former roommate of, Gabe – now Fast's roommate – and all three were pals. Andra asked Fast and me to play at her birthday party at Disco 2000, the big Wednesday night weirdo-techno, club-kid night at Limelight. It was hosted by Michael Alig, who later became an infamous murderer, but that's a whole other story.

Disco 2000 was packed with about three thousand strange-ass wonderful people every week. I was working there that night anyway, so when it was time for us to do the show, I checked that the bars under my responsibility were stocked up, punched out on the time clock and got changed. I put on some borrowed Adidas Superstars and a bright blue down parka. I was a very slight version of my former Marine weight, so I beefed it up with the puffy coat.

The gig was only a few songs. Three, to be exact. The first song was titled 'Passive/Aggressive' and had a rock guitar in the chorus which got everyone's attention. The vocals were a rap verse that I kept short and punchy, and then we hit them with the singalong chorus over a chopped-up guitar riff from the band Helmet. That went down better than I had expected, and seeing that this was all just a huge experiment, I rode the wave.

The next song was called 'King of New York'. I had written the chorus to 'King of New York' as one of my first attempts at rap lyric writing. 'La-di da-di' was a phrase that is in every hip-hop lover's lexicon, and if you were from New York City it went even deeper, almost to the cellular level. So when I alloyed that with the legend of the 'Teflon Don', John Gotti, I hit a vein of something that got to these people that night.

The crowd was actually having a good time at the expense of their techno rave birthday soiree. It was trippy: rather than throwing stuff at us like I thought they would, by the end of the song they were singing the '*La-di da-di*' line along with us.

The fact that the sound guys at the Limelight were as good as it got in all of New York City didn't hurt. They were close friends of ours and made sure at soundcheck that we had everything we needed. During the show, I could see by how the crowd was bopping their heads along with the beats that we had some serious shit, sound wise, going on. The bass was vibrating the whole stage and knocking over drinks that people had rested on the edge.

The best part of being in a band is being loud. Not annoyingly loud, shrill and ear-splitting, but powerful. I thought the sound we made as a band had a warmth to it that was relayed to the crowd that night. That's why they were bugging out and having fun: we were giving them the sonic diet they were used to, just on a different dish. The actual frequencies we used to make our music sound 'good' was a great low end and careful equalisation of higher stuff to make it all a cohesive sound. That was translated to the audience and we took that back to our recordings. We were careful in remembering what moved a crowd at Limelight when we mixed our stuff, initially. The sounds and beats and cultural relevance of the impact of the track were super important, but what everything rested on was the bass.

'No joke, the bass got us over. I mean, we got us over, but there was some bass god watching over us that night, amen.' Having stood up to recount the gig, I had resumed my seat on Joyce's sofa across from her chair. As relieved as I was about the gig being over, describing it to Joyce was raising my blood pressure.

'Amen.' Joyce knew just what to say.

'The last song was a cover of Joe Walsh.' I looked at Joyce closely here to see if she recognized Joe Walsh's name.

'The Eagle?' Joyce knew her stuff.

'Yeah, that guy.' I winked at her and she winked back. 'He did a song back in the day about being a rock star and all the bullshit funny stuff like losing your driving licence and wrecking hotel rooms . . .'

I let that one ring out to see if she was tracking.

'Anyway,' she deadpanned me. Joyce had great comedic timing.

'Anyway, it had a really cool breakdown that we made a feature of the song. And the crowd ate it up.'

I was still trying to convince myself of the night's success, and by retelling my account I could see how unbelievable this all sounded. But it actually happened and I was responsible for it, and that was the hold-up on my end. I had a huge problem giving myself props. I was always my own worst enemy. I can't seem to give myself any credit. Rest assured I have already wrestled that alligator a few times. I just have an inferiority complex that I know is bullshit, but even through all that rationalization, it still manifests itself in my negative self-talk. I was working on stopping this dumb shit, but it was a deep program glitch that I had to root out, and that took time and hard work to tackle the problem head on.

Joyce knew all this as well. While I was running my mouth she was looking at me like I was the best thing since sliced bread.

'The song ends,' I continued the story, 'and everyone on the balcony surrounding the stage, Andra and all her club-kid friends and shit, they're clapping and yelling. The rest of the main room, which is full of maybe three thousand weirdoes, they're bugging out too!'

Joyce was holding her hands together like an excited child as I recounted the night.

'The really cool thing was after the DJ started to play the techno music again the crowd kept cheering for us . . .'

I was reminded of how I felt at that moment. A sense of accomplishment I hadn't felt since the Marines. A sense that I had overcome and improvised and ultimately adapted to my situation on that stage and . . . won. I won a battle. It was an important win for me and I needed to give myself these flowers and stop all the negativity. 'I did it, Joyce.' I said it tired, like I had finished a marathon, not like I had just kicked some ass.

'Yes you did, Huey.'

I knew Joyce understood my mental situation better than anyone, but I had to say it out loud to her anyway. I tried not to sound melodramatic but it was difficult. 'I'm so happy I didn't kill myself all those times I thought I didn't have any hope of getting here . . .' I looked around the room for something to distract me from the heart of the matter. But nothing stuck because nothing could come close to what I was about to finally realize. This was the thing I would remember about the first gig.

I now had something to live for.

Me.

Chapter Ten

Angie

A ngie and I were becoming closer and closer. I would still hang at her place most days and blaze joints when her kid Isabella was at school. The exception was Tuesday evenings, when her boyfriend came by. He was a 'made' guy from 'downtown' who Angie had been with since forever. They had an agreement that every Tuesday he would come and spend the night. I wasn't to bother her, no one could; even Isabella had to go to a friend's place and stay over.

Angie continued to help me out with the catering gigs at the private members' club downtown in the financial district. We carried on smoking joints on our breaks and laughing at the Wall Street bros. I soon figured Angie really was knee deep in the 'Life'. I knew better than to pry and did my best to stay out of most of it, but – damn! – it sounded like fun.

It was hard, though, not to pick up on what was going on. With all the time Angie and I spent together, and from what I witnessed (bad choice of words) she appeared to be working with a crew that had a hustle that involved cash. That cash was sometimes dropped off and picked up by nefarious types, but I never really asked exactly what was going on.

Although all the comings and goings began to make me a little nervous. One afternoon, after watching a 'Westie' drop off what looked like a huge amount of cash in a brown paper bag, I asked Angie about it.

'Honey, this is a weigh station.' She passed me a joint and gave me her knowing wink. '████ gave me this gig to run because no one would ever rob me because of who he is. I've kept it going with no fuck-ups because of who I am.'

I nodded and processed the hustle. 'Do you get a cut?' I asked.

Angie looked at the bag and then back at me. 'Boy, you are bold,' she said, turning serious. The edge in Angie's voice left me feeling like I had been somewhat impolite.

'Sorry to ask. I'm not sure why I did. Curiosity and cats don't mix.'

'No, honey, they don't.' Angie was lightening up a little now, the flash of annoyance leaving her voice. 'If I thought I couldn't trust you I wouldn't have let you see what's up, *capisce?*'

'Yeah,' I managed. I tried to process what Angie was telling me, and why she was letting me in. I worried that she was allowing me to see this part of her life because she wanted me to be involved in some way. I decided to make clear I wasn't interested. 'You know, this stuff really isn't what I want to get myself involved in anymore.'

Angie did her best scoff. 'Baby, that's not why I told you about what I do.'

I was confused again as to why she was showing me these things she was up to.

As it turned out, I wasn't to be confused for long.

'Huey, ▮▮▮▮ and I are looking at maybe getting indicted on a RICO case the feds are bringing against the crew ▮▮▮▮ runs downtown. We heard from the lawyers we have in the courts that it's gonna be a wide net.'

Shit. I was nodding like I knew what she was talking about, but I did not know exactly what was being said. (Other than a RICO case is federal law: the Racketeer Influenced and Corrupt Organizations Act.)

'I know you know what kinda heat the feds can bring to the party,' Angie continued. 'And I'm not trying to drag you into any of that.' She was a changed woman all of a sudden. The confident, brash Angie I knew had disappeared. This Angie was scared, you could tell. I had never seen that before. 'It's Izzy . . .'

Her daughter. 'Is she in trouble too?' I was fond of the kid and hoped the feds would leave her out of it. She was 16 and was basically still just a kid. Angie was very protective of her daughter, and it was this that I assumed was the source of her fear.

'If I get pinched and have to go into custody to await trial Isabella would be put into foster care right off the bat.' Angie was scared that the feds would leverage Izzy's freedom to encourage her to flip on ▄▄▄▄ and his alleged unlawful activity. 'If it's a longer stretch . . . well, I'm no rat, so that's leaving Izzy exposed, um . . .'

I could tell from the pauses that Angie was about to tell me something. I sat back and let her get to it in her own time, trying not to rush her.

'Isabella is 16 now,' Angie explained. 'If she was somehow legally married she would become an "emancipated minor" and no longer under the jurisdiction of the courts if I wasn't around. They would not be able to put her into foster care with god knows who. Huey, I could face the charge and not get squeezed by these fucking rats . . .' Angie looked away. She was angry and upset at the situation, crying real tears of frustration. She had a little moment where I had to give her a hug to chill her out.

'I'll do it,' I said to her head in my arms.

Angie looked up at me, still crying, 'What?'

'I'll do it . . . I'll marry her to keep her safe.'

'You will? Why?' Angie had stopped crying and was now genuinely surprised. 'Why would you offer to do that for me?' Her eyes were shining, and locked on to mine.

'Because . . . because I can.'

Angie smiled what seemed to be her most beautiful smile. She was fighting back more tears, but I could tell these were a different kind. 'Huey, that's the nicest thing anyone has ever offered to do for me. But you really can't say that, can you?'

'Of course I can.' I was now over my initial reservation of offering my hand in marriage. I had no obligations to anyone, I didn't have to move in with her, it would be fine. The more I had time to think it through, the more I figured it wouldn't be too much of a hassle. 'I don't have a family of my own yet,' I explained, 'and you have been such a great friend to me that I figure I can. So please let me repay you some of the loyalty you've shown me.'

'Come here, kid,' Angie grabbed me and gave me a big hug filled with relief and affection.

Chapter Eleven

The Bail Scene

It wasn't too long after I married Angie's kid, Isabella, that Angie got pinched. Just like she told me she would.

I got a call on my little cellphone from Angie's boyfriend's driver. He told me she got arrested in the big RICO sweep. The sweep was the doing of the bulls from the SDNY (Southern District of New York) that was the federal authorities' law enforcement racket. The SDNY's old boss was an Italian from the neighbourhood named Rudy Giuliani, who was now mayor of New York City. Before being elected mayor Rudy had dedicated his life to sticking it to the mafia. The way he saw it, the mafia disparaged every honest Italian American by participating in the exploitation of immigrants, the proliferation of violence and, funnily, propagating 'negative stereotypes'. Italians in the New York mafia respected Rudy because he was from the culture. But they also hated him for what he was doing and had done to the Five Families.

He put away more goodfellas than any other New York City DA ever had, and that resonated with the boys downtown.

Angie had got pinched on a Thursday evening, which meant she probably wouldn't get to see a judge until the following afternoon. Manhattan's criminal courts used to run all night long, but not so much anymore. The guy on the phone told me that within the next two hours I was going to get over to Hell's Kitchen to pick up a 'package', which I would then deliver to another guy downtown. I knew the job had something to do with Angie getting arrested but from how these guys were acting there was obviously more to this errand. I was told that I would know both guys, which was cool. I asked if I could take my friend Mateo along with me, both for his car and for another set of hands if needed.

Mateo had been helping me run some errands for Angie lately, so this was no big deal. Over the last few months I had been helping Angie out here and there and whenever she was short of a delivery guy, she'd ask me to get my 'nice friend from Jersey' to drive me. The packages we delivered were always money, or at least that was my assumption: I never actually looked inside them.

The funny thing with all this was that Mateo's little cousin, Kevin the Kid, was dating Isabella secretly behind all of our backs the whole time. Well, most of our backs. Angie, of course, knew everything. When Mateo would come into the city in his pearl white Volkswagen Jetta, Kevin the Kid would tag along. He'd get out and give me the front seat, all respectful, then hang around Angie's apartment and smoke weed with her until we came back. Which is how he met Isabella. Kids being kids, their eyes must have met and shit must have happened.

The first thing Mateo did on picking me up, me having put him in the frame on the ride west, was to ask if I had eaten.

'Nah,' I yawned. 'I just got up when the guy called, and then I called you . . .' Mateo was always so fucking chipper that sometimes it really annoyed me.

'I knew you wouldn't have had a chance to get a meal.' He smiled annoyingly at his own reflection in the rear-view, but I forgave him for what he said next. 'I made a Tupperware with some braised swordfish I made at work and some homemade linguini in a red sauce . . . it's kinda spicy.'

As well as working as a DJ, Mateo also worked as a line chef. He had started in the 'wop joints' as he called them, out in the middle of nowhere New Jersey. Mateo had started washing dishes for money to buy records. As he'd graduated to cooking, so his DJing had progressed into 'off the books' gigs in Manhattan. Sometime soon he was going to have to choose between the two.

Mateo was moving one hand behind himself to rummage on the back seat, kissing his lips like a real-life chef with the other. I turned around in my seat to help him before he crashed the car. I found the Tupperware box and put it on my lap. It was warm and smelled amazing.

'I warmed it up on half-power in the microwave,' Mateo explained. He always went on and on about how microwave ovens suck and if you absolutely must use one half-power was required, even though you had to put it in for twice as long. 'Forks in the glove box, linen in the door panel,' Mateo directed, before lamenting, 'I didn't bring wine.' He wasn't visibly upset at saying this, but he was disappointed, for sure. He broke into his best French accent. '*Bon appetite*, motherfucker . . .'

As I enjoyed possibly the best, and definitely the first, spicy swordfish and linguini I'd eaten, Mateo sped on towards a particularly dark corner of Hell's Kitchen.

We pulled up at the 'Westy' guy's address that I'd been given on the phone. I was expecting to get out, bullshit with the guy for five minutes before he gave me the package and we bailed. Instead, he saw us and just jumped in the back seat. 'Yo, Huey. You good, cuz?'

We will call this guy Irish. He was mid-thirties, longish black hair in a ponytail with a black jeans ensemble that wouldn't get a second look at a Johnny Cash concert or on a stylish Paris street.

'Yeah, Irish; copacetic, mano,' I replied. 'Why are you in the car, though? You need a ride?' I might have been smiling but this guy worried me. Irish was a well-known psycho and having him in our car increased the likelihood of us attracting some kind of tail. That sucked and all, but particularly when we still had a mission to try to pull off.

Irish just laughed. 'Huey, baby. I love you but this is a lot of money.' He held up a Power Memorial High School gym bag, which through the canvas you could see was stuffed with tight bricks of cash. I reckoned it looked like 40 to 50 grand, but I would've had to hold it to see how much it weighed to be sure. I couldn't tell the denominations of the bills, and with gambling receipts there's a lot of fives and tens thrown in to make up the total. So, you know, half a million in hundred-dollar bills weighs just over ten pounds, ten-and-one-quarter pounds, to be exact, not taking into consideration the bag. I eyed Irish while he was eyeing me, and then we both eyed Mateo who nodded his head at the Tupperware bowl on the seat next to Irish.

'You hungry, Irish?' I asked.

On the drive south on the West Side Highway, Irish filled us in while eating what was left of the pasta, one of Mateo's linen napkins sticking out of his shirt collar. He told us what Angie had told him from her call from the Tombs. (That's what they call MCC, the Metropolitan Correctional Center.) 'Angie just told me that they heard them coming into the restaurant.' He saluted Mateo with his fork, 'This is lovely, Mateo, thank you.' Mateo smiled in the rear-view and then looked over at me like I was giving him a look, which I wasn't. 'They had a few extra minutes because they were eating in the back room,' Irish continued, leaning his head towards the open window and moving his face in and out of the jet stream like a dog would.

I was nervous enough having this guy in the car, but now I could tell he was high as well. We couldn't get downtown soon enough as far as I was concerned. I gave Mateo a nudge when I thought I could do so unseen, but Irish somehow saw it.

'Relax, bro, I'm just along for the ride to make sure the guineas don't forget whose money this is.' Irish moved back his black oxford shirt, to show me his pistol in his waist. It was a small 9mm single-stack magazine, a girl's gun.

'I'm cool bro,' I managed, trying to light a cigarette in the breeze.

Mateo, who had noticed the change in tone quickly got us back on track. 'Hey, do you girls like house music?'

He hit the Blaupunkt stereo in the Jetta and the bass went boom! We all laughed a little too loud, but it got us all reset and put our heads back in the moment as to why we were there. To help Angie.

The rest was noise, or house music.

When we neared the club house where Angie's boyfriend's crew hung out, Mateo pulled over and I called my contact from a pay phone. The plan hadn't been given to me in one fell swoop: I was only being told what I was supposed to do from moment to moment, so when the guy told me where to go next, I did. He said to come by an apartment they used for meetings and we would then get all the cash together. The apartment was just off from the famous Five Points area of Lower Manhattan, where the notorious gangs of New York fought for local dominance. There was even a little plaque about it by the park on the corner, which was where Mateo parked up. He stayed in the car while Irish and I headed for the handover.

When you're transporting large amounts of cash through an urban area the best way to do it is quickly. Don't pause in front of buildings, on corners and never in a hallway. That's where ambushes are set up: in a hallway, there is no place to get out of the way of a bullet. I gave Irish a nod to say I knew this was the dangerous part. He nodded back, moving his suit jacket clear of his waistband where his little lady gun was. I wasn't armed with a gun, just the flat head screwdriver I always kept in my back pocket. As I rang the buzzer for apartment 4C I made sure it was still there. It's not like I really believed a screwdriver was going to help me in a gunfight, but it made me feel good enough to push the door open when the buzzer sounded.

As the door clicked shut behind, Irish and I waited and listened. If some guys were gonna do something, this was where the ambush would happen. I felt for my screwdriver again, but nobody came. We knew after a few seconds that it wasn't a set-up. I turned to Irish, put my hand up and pointed at the ceiling. '4 C,' I said.

We took the stairs two at a time to burn off the adrenaline that had been dumped into our bodies in anticipation of the potential fight for our lives. The fourth floor was the penultimate floor of the building. On the landing we smelled some really nice cooking, and I thought it wasn't such a bad stereotype to have: Italians being good in the kitchen. Maybe we were just in time for lunch.

Less than a second after ringing the doorbell it was opened up by a young handsome Italian American in a Don Mattingly jersey. Don Mattingly is a New York Yankee legend: captain of the team for many years when the Yankees won a whole bunch of championships. The guy in the Mattingly jersey we'll call Jerry. I knew him pretty well and he greeted me with a grin. 'Huey, my good man. Come on in . . .' He saw Irish behind me and before I made any introductions they both started groaning like old women.

'Jesus, Jerry, Mattingly? Really? The fucking guy is a garbage first baseman,' said Irish.

Jerry did not give a fuck about that cheap shot and got right to it. 'It' being Irish's bad hygiene: 'You smelly mick fuck. You waddle in here like a Saint Paddy's reject with all that money? The "yams" shoulda robbed you outside.'

Irish laughed and mentioned that it was rare to see anyone other than Italians around this neighbourhood. 'The only thing I'm worried about outside on the street is your sister!'

I took this as friendly banter and left them to it to look around the pad. From the clear plastic runners that formed a path over the paisley carpets, it was a loaner, for sure. There were clear plastic slip covers on the sofa and the matching chair, an affectation that a lot of immigrant home-makers got into to protect the furnishings. It reminded me of my old friend Eddie Velardi's house, whose mom was hyper vigilant when it came to keeping the abode clean. The lamps on the end tables had little drops of oil cascading down the sides, which I had never seen before. They gave off a golden light that made everything look like the 1970s. I lit a cigarette and watched the two gangsters do their dance for a while. When they seemed more settled I walked back over to the coffee table where they were standing. They had frozen looking tough at each other, but my presence broke the spell.

'Big boy Huey!' Jerry put his hand on my shoulder. 'You're good to drop all this to Angie's mouthpiece?'

I followed his eyes to the table, where there were now two gym bags, the Power Memorial one and a brown leather bag that had Pierre Cardin written in script on the side.

'Sure. I'd like to be able to put it all into to one bag, though. Easier to handle.' I was thinking about when I left there, and how it would just be me and Mateo. If shit got thick, it was easier to look after one bag of cash than it is two.

'Smart kid.' Jerry nodded and headed towards the bedrooms, where he opened a closet in the hallway. 'My aunt has a bunch of D'Agostino bags – they work for you?'

He was talking to me but Irish answered, 'Is it a plastic bag, Jerry?'

'Who the fuck asked your highness?' Jerry snapped back. 'Yeah I said it, what?'

Irish had a look on his face that needed no interpreting. 'You fucking mutt,' he blurted. 'I'll—'

'Those bags are fine, Jerry,' I jumped in, mostly to save my own life but also to remind the guys that we were supposed to be helping Angie get out of custody. I tapped Irish on the arm to get his attention. 'Here, help me get these two bags open and out on the table . . .' Irish looked back and forth from me to Jerry, sucking his teeth loudly. 'Motherfuckers,' he sighed, and opened the Power Memorial bag onto the glass coffee table. As the cash cascaded onto the table, I bent over to grab a wad that fell to the floor. It was ten grand in a rubber band. There was way more than 50 here, maybe the cash was for more than Angie's bail. I didn't ask.

When I had put both batches of cash into the D'Agostino grocery bag (which I doubled up to be safe) Jerry told me he was going to text me the lawyer's address and contact number and started typing. When Jerry told me the guy's name Irish spoke up: 'What about the judge's parking attendant? Wasn't he going to do that thing?'

This was getting a little heavy for me to be hearing. What in the world had a 'judge's parking attendant' got to do with any of this? Was I becoming a part of a conspiracy to do some really bad shit?

Jerry shook his head at Irish like he was retarded: 'That was a bad idea. We decided that that plan was . . . unwise.'

My mom didn't raise a dummy, so I took that as my cue to grab the plastic grocery bag full of cash off the coffee table and make to go. 'Ok, well, if that's settled?' I looked from Irish to Jerry and back. They both nodded at me and that was that. I left them staring at each other in the borrowed apartment. I took the plastic grocery bag filled with cash, skipped down the four flights of stairs and got back into Mateo's Jetta as quickly as I could. 'Them boys are crazy,' I exhaled.

'Where to now?' Mateo put the car into first gear.

I looked at my phone and read the address out loud. 'Metropolitan Correctional Center. It's on Park Row, right behind the courthouse on Foley Square. You know it?'

Mateo nodded, 'Yeah, I know it. Do we have time to grab a bite?'

Chapter Twelve

The Joyce Debrief Scene

From Joyce's office on 10th Street, the New York skyline looked burnished in the late afternoon autumn light. The East Village in all her glory lay before us. It was a majestic view that took in all the best parts of Lower Manhattan minus the fluff of the World Trade Center that was due south, past our particular frame. It always filled me up.

I was familiar with the view by now. I was beginning to get myself back together, and that was thanks to Joyce being kind enough to let me restore my bearing. Even so, there were still issues that I needed to resolve, and today I was there to discuss a particular one.

Belisa.

Up until now I had thought of her as my girl. I loved her. I was faithful and protected her however I could without question. She was a good woman deep down, and I based all the stuff she had been fronting on me with through that lens.

She wanted the best for me and was putting herself in the future with me, and I took that as a considered compliment.

I'm no love-sick puppy but when someone tells me they love me – because no more than a handful of people have ever told me that my whole life – I feel a deep sense of gratitude. It comes from being abandoned as a kid by my father; and then later when my mom got remarried; and then again when I got separated from the Marines and cast adrift without any love shown for my loyalty.

I took what we had together seriously. But I was still me, and didn't like the 'just-go-get-a-job-at-UPS-and-stop-all-this-fussin'-with-those-two-losers' bullshit I was being forced to hear every time we were together. Our conversations always seemed to devolve at some juncture to her asking me to assess my current mental state and rethink what I was up against. Who, she'd ask, would gamble everything they had, their time and their youth, on such a small success window? 'And then what?' she would ask rhetorically.

Belisa hated Fast and thought our music was dumb, but she was from some Rockland County suburb where they don't know shit about music. So I let her comments slide, but that made something inside me angry at her.

For all of Belisa's comments, my music was going great. It felt like it was just where I could see it, which I know sure sounds pretentious, but I could literally hold a demo tape that represented the Fun Lovin' Criminals as we were.

And then there were the awesome random gigs we'd been performing around the three clubs Peter Gatien owned. They were kind of spaced out, time wise, maybe a month or two between them, but these gigs had made us a name.

Belisa saw things differently. My answers, she'd tell me, were feeble attempts at protecting my bruised and battered ego. I would tend to believe her when she'd tell me how fucked up I was, and that made something inside me furious, for rubbing my face in it. I hoped she loved me as much as she told me she did before she began her sermons. I had tuned her out of late but I was feeling lonely and that makes men do dumb shit. But using some charm and regularly seeing Joyce, I had gotten it all sweet again between us.

Belisa believed in Joyce as much as I did. If Joyce was cool with my progress then so was she – for the time being. Which was why I had just gotten a last-minute session in with Joyce before I had to go to Puerto Rico with Belisa in the hope of continuing to rekindle whatever we still had together.

'I'm sorry, Joyce. My dumb ass doesn't know which way to go but out.' I had sand in my socks and tears in my eyes. Leaving me reduced to reliving past trauma while shedding survivor's guilt all alloyed with a sense of personal relief.

I had just told Joyce of how the band was getting a big break by being asked to play at one of the big Sunday night

Limelight rock and roll nights. This was a huge deal as the promoter had asked for us by name, not by, 'Who the fuck can fill in at the last second?' After a few hard years doing all this nefarious shit to keep my dream alive, it was too much for my poor heart to take anymore and I was tripping out.

I felt safe around Joyce, which allowed me to become emotional around her. I always felt that I was too much to be around at those moments, but Joyce was a tough cookie. She has the kindest face and was giving me a pat on the hand that was shaking on my knee.

I looked up through the tears and suddenly a weird laughter began from deep inside me. This kind of stuff happens after you get into a tight spot and you live to experience the feeling of the adrenaline leaving your blood system as fast as it came into it. The absurdity of life – how fragile we all are; how crazy it is to live through whatever gave you that sweet adrenaline blast in the first place – that was the thought process this time.

You hear about dudes becoming adrenaline junkies after a hitch in some hairy military outfit, and I totally get it. Right after I got out, I signed up for the New York Fire Academy. Where else could a guy like me with an honourable discharge get a job where your life was not assured, you did good for your community, and you didn't need a heater? Yep, the New York City Fire Department: 'New York's Bravest!' I liked the moniker as well; who didn't love a fireman?

Above: Steve and I in the studio.

Left: Me in my hotel room in St. Louis before our first U2 show.

Below: Sugar at home.

Above: Me onstage
in Dublin at Eamon
Doran's pub.

Right and below: More
pics of me and the band
in Dublin.

Above: Backstage at Leeds festival, 1999.

Right: My first ever advance check from EMI.

MY FIRST ROYALTY/ADVANCE CHECK

Left: Tuning up onstage in 1996.

Below: Mateo at soundcheck, 1995.

After I bleached my hair at my girlfriend's house.

My roommate Chris and I at the Beacon theatre in NYC.

Me in the liquor room of Club USA, 1993.

Me playing live at The Tunnel nightclub, 1995.

My Hawaiian boys on Maui, 1998.

The FLC circa 1994.

Mike Schnapp and FLC at the U2 show at the Meadowlands 1996.

In Joyce's presence, I had a feeling that I hadn't planned for. I felt a weird sense of gratitude. After all the bullshit I'd had to endure, I was making progress. I could see it and so could my people. They told me how I was looking different, holding myself in a way they hadn't seen before. My attitude was now geared towards success and making a life in music. I was focused and had a real tangible goal. All the tough times – the times I had to list to myself the few reasons I shouldn't kill myself; the times I walked on the Brooklyn Bridge without my dog Sugar knowing I was in a dark place and maybe wouldn't make it back home – all that crazy shit didn't get me. I felt as if I had defeated something sinister inside, a devil that wanted me to fail and be miserable. A demon that wanted my death.

Well, fuck that shit. I wasn't going to let that dark negative stuff kill me.

Joyce could sense something in me shifting and asked, 'Are you winning the battle, my dear?'

I looked up and met her eye. 'I think I am.' I smiled and took an inventory of sorts. 'I mean, I'm not losing myself in the dark stew of my past, and that's something . . .' I laughed. 'The part that's most mystifying is that I still feel guilt. A guilt for not dying.'

I stopped laughing as my high-flying mood hit some turbulence. There has always been survivor's guilt to deal with. My feelings along those lines were typical of a guy who'd made it through while others didn't, but what made my guilt acute was how it manifested itself. I felt a sense of obligation to look after the guys in my inner circle like they were my Marine brothers in a firefight. Fast, Steve, Mateo . . . even Angie got this treatment. I was obsessive about their safety and wellbeing. I felt that I had to live up to some expectation about how my life should be, in honour of those men who didn't have that chance. I think that's what Joyce was seeing in me from her perch on the sofa.

I had a few loose ends flying around inside my head and I took a few more moments to arrange them so I could articulate them to Joyce. When I did, I continued my debrief: 'So, I'm kinda good with all the real old, mother, father stuff now, mainly because it didn't kill me . . .' I smiled at Joyce so she wouldn't think I'd completely flipped my lid. 'It's a new chapter in my life, right? The band is doing its thing, I'm finally getting a handle on all this . . .' I raised my hands around us both to signify our therapy sessions.

Joyce smiled and nodded her encouragement.

'And if I can finesse this girlfriend of mine to ease back on the whole "plan B/go-get-a-job-at-UPS"' – Joyce smiled at that because she knew how much Belisa had chopped my onions about giving up on my dream and getting a real job – 'I might, just might, be able to call this year a very good one, after all.'

I had a sudden feeling that I hadn't thanked Joyce for all she'd done to get me to this point, and I made a ponderous effort to correct my error. 'You know that I wouldn't be here without you.' I levelled my eyes at her, letting her know this wasn't bullshit, that I was being strictly sincere.

Joyce smiled again, and waved her hand to dismiss my thought. 'No, my dear, I just helped you see a few things that were in your blind spot.'

'There's a big difference between having a blind spot and being fucking blind, Joyce!'

We both laughed at this. But I wasn't finished. 'Joyce, you know that I don't have anyone who really . . .'

'I know, my dear, you don't have to say it.'

Joyce was such a cool person to help me out. I mean, who the fuck was I? Some crusty vet. A serious head-case that no one in their right mind would want to help, that's who. I didn't deserve Joyce and that's what I was trying to get at. I didn't deserve any of the good fortune I was basking in now, but I was smart enough to know that it wasn't a bad thing to let it ride. 'All things must pass' is a saying I think about a lot when things get bad. There's a Bible passage from Corinthians that sums it up nicely: 'For these light and momentary troubles are preparing us for an eternal glory that far outweighs them all . . .'

But the idea that these unexpected good things would also pass into the abyss as well, like tears in the rain, made me want to tell Joyce how I felt even more. 'It's been hard not having a family to talk to . . . but you've become as close to family as I can imagine, Joyce, and I want you to know how much I appreciate your time and patience . . .' I was trying to jam everything I wanted to tell her into one sentence, and I paused when it was clear I was failing to do that well.

Joyce took this as her cue to get me off 'the X'. That's an expression that we used in the Marines when you were exposed and needed to get to a safe place. 'Huey, you do most of the heavy lifting yourself.' She made a face like a dismissive Frenchman. 'I just tell you where the heavy stuff has settled and you're the one that goes in there – by yourself, I might add – and sorts it out.'

Joyce said that last part like she was proud of me for doing that. What else could I have done? Ignored everything and just kept going? No, I would have had to have faced it all, she knew that. I'm not scared of dying anymore because I've already accepted that I'm only here on a temporary basis. When I think about how far I'd come in just a few months, how I changed my whole program, I couldn't have done it without Joyce.

'Listen, kiddo,' I called her that as a nickname because she was so little. 'You can tell me that I'm the one being brave here. But without you helping me see that I can change how I think, shit . . .' I trailed off the obvious point. We didn't need to say the word suicide again to understand what

I was really saying. She saved my life. I knew it, and now she knew that I knew it too. I would have been long gone if I hadn't been able to change the way my mind was working. She helped me do that and I was forever grateful to her.

'My band is playing shows! I'm up front rocking my guitar! Damn, Joyce! I wouldn't have ever thought this would have been possible before we met . . .' I began to get misty again. The feeling I had was one of gratitude, with a side of shame. Shame is a worthless emotion – it gives nothing but takes whatever you let it take: self-esteem, self-confidence, whatever. I felt shame because I still felt unworthy deep down. Unworthy of all the blessings I was receiving. I still had some deep issues to resolve about my father, and the idea of me not being worthy of my musical success was the hardest to understand. I'd worked for years to get really good on guitar and years more getting a working understanding of multi-track recording, but there remained a shadow over me. The shadow moved away from time to time, but it was never gone for too long. Joyce helped me spot that shadow and sometimes even helped me avoid it entirely. 'Joyce . . .' I couldn't form the words, but the sentiment was clear enough to her.

'It's ok, Huey,' she placed a hand on my shoulder. 'You'll get there.'

'Where, Joyce?' I asked earnestly wiping my face with the back of my hand.

'Your life, my dear,' she answered. 'Your beautiful life.'

Chapter Thirteen

The Night We Got Signed

When we did our seventh or eighth show at the Limelight, our homeboy and resident Limelight VIP Room DJ, Dominic DeLuca, brought someone along to see us play. Unbeknownst to us, Dom, as well as being DJ at the club's Sunday night rock and roll party, worked as a scout. Mike Schnapp had just gotten the job of VP of A&R at EMI Records and had put the word out to his sources to feed him some possible bands to sign. We were lucky with the timing. This was right about the time that bands like Korn and the Deftones were popping off in what the music journalists liked to call the 'nu-metal' scene.

The Limelight had them come through and they were all big hip-hop fans. This revelation brought a lot more hip-hop music into the Sunday night lexicon at the Limelight. Through that we got the call to open up for bands like these. Though the crowd on Sundays were diehard rockers, living in NYC in the nineties made you a hip-hop fan by default. Everywhere you went in the city, the new hip-hop revolution was happening. Huge brands were now embracing the culture and its young stars were now going mainstream. Media was eating up everything 'bling' and covering rap beef like a global summit meeting. Bands like Cypress Hill were crossing the line, with fans of all backgrounds making our kind of hybrid a viable new lane. Having the hip-hop and the rock-guitar elements at the forefront of our sound didn't hurt our chances at all.

When Mike Schnapp saw us open up for Korn after hearing our demo tape he liked us so much that he told his boss, EMI Chairman Davitt Sigerson, all about this new band that were taking downtown by storm. Davitt was a record producer as well as the CEO of a major label, and his taste was what the US part of EMI Records had wanted running the label. Turned out he loved our demo too. Mike also asked Dom to let him know when our next gig was so he could bring Davitt down to it.

That gig took place in the smallish 'VIP Room' of the Limelight. The VIP Room was on the top floor and was meant to hold about a hundred, but we'd packed it with about a hundred more. We had been getting some buzz from our recent shows mainly because the gigs were openers for big acts and a lot of people saw us there. We'd also packed the place with all of our friends who either hung out or worked at the clubs.

There was a real excitement in the club that night. We were all hanging out and getting loose before the show when Dom bounded in and quickly sobered us all up. Dom was a long-haired metal-head BMX dude who had this fucked-up pinky finger on his right hand from a bike accident that made it look dislocated when he waved it around, which he did whenever he got excited. It was flapping all over the place now and that told me he was a little nervous for us.

'Yo, Huey, I just wanted you to know that there are a few very heavy people in the crowd tonight.'

I guessed he hoped we wouldn't blow it and mess up his reputation. But I didn't get nervous. I was a United States Marine, for Christ's sake: playing a few songs to a few hundred unarmed civilians wasn't the thing to raise my blood pressure.

Besides, this gig was going to be really special because of all the people I had worked with over the years who were showing their love by supporting us. I thought at best we would get some interest from the label, whoever 'they' might be. I was worried we would be pressured to change the sound or succumb to some commercial bullshit suggestion, and I knew I wasn't going for any of that. Even so, I was secretly pleased that the few shows we had done were good enough for the 'record executives' to catch the buzz. We were trying something new, a formula that was unique to us and our time, and the powers that be wanted to come and hear us for themselves.

That night, I know we played most of the songs that made up our first album, but I can't remember much about the actual performance. What I do remember is that all of our friends went absolutely crazy when we came onstage and kept that energy up for the whole set. They looked so proud of us, and that left a very lasting impression on me. That meant so much to me, their pride that we might break free and make it.

Our crowd were a bunch of club-kid rejects and counter-culture types who chose to live on the margins, supporting us and acting as megaphones for our new sound. They promoted us to their communities back home in and around the city's suburbs, away from the clubs in Manhattan, where the real people lived. Thanks to them, the demos we made were getting played on small college radio shows and on the occasional community public access cable TV show. We had a following among the disenfranchised of New York City and it was cool to see how they rode for us in the early days.

The way they all went crazy that night when we started to play set the tone for our set. I believe their reaction gave the bigwigs in attendance the inclination to make us an offer the moment we got offstage. The jokes I cracked between songs were met with outrageous laughter and applause, so much so I even felt at one point our friends were pouring it on a bit strong with the outrageous responses.

After the gig we were putting our gear away and drinking the free beer when the door of the dressing room opened and Dom popped his smiling head in. This time he didn't look so nervous. 'Fellas! That was amazing, no joke, so fucking good! La-di da-di, Huey, you crazy motherfucker . . .'

He stepped aside for a few guys behind him, who were also smiling. As they came into the room, Dom introduced us: 'Guys, this is Mike Schnapp.' Dom presented a big man of about 35 with long hair and a beard à la Rick Rubin wearing a Slayer t-shirt and red suede Puma Clydes. Mike gave us a cool handshake and said how much he liked the show, but he kept it short. He did that because the guy behind him with the white linen shirt open at the collar, yellow-gold Rolex Day-Date and air of authority had put his left hand out to me. In it was a business card. I took the card in my left hand and began to read it . . . 'Davitt Sigerson CEO of EMI Records'.

As I got to the CEO bit his right hand met mine and we shook. I looked up to meet his eye and he was grinning. This was a new level of slickness. He knew exactly what he was doing. At that moment I knew my life had changed forever, Davitt actually squeezed my hand. He was sharing this moment of excitement with me, and it was genuine. 'My name is Davitt Sigerson,' he continued to shake my hand. 'Would you like to make a record?'

Like in all big moments in your life, everything slowed down. I saw the blue smoke from my joint trace past the dressing-room spotlight that was pointed to the ceiling. I could hear my own heart beat. I felt a new feeling for the first time and it felt strange. Was it vindication? Vindication for all the sacrifices I had made to be good at this music thing, all the hard work and compulsion to make music no matter the cost? 'Yes, I really would. Thanks, Davitt, it's nice to meet you too.'

I had always had a feeling that I would be able to achieve what I had set out to do. But I hadn't expected it to be so resounding a result.

Davitt, Mike and the rest of us talked for a few minutes about the music and how we performed it. Davitt was very interested in the process. We agreed to meet up the next day at the EMI offices to talk more about our impending deal. As they left, I tried to get my head round what had just happened. Someone had discovered me, like in the movies, and it was hard to process.

The next day I took Steve and James 'Jimmy', our ersatz manager, up to 1290 Avenue of the Americas for the big meeting at the EMI offices. Fast had bailed on us and took some chick to Florida for some fun in the sun, so I was left to lead the band into uncharted territories.

We were thoroughly checked through security in the lobby and then took an elevator the size of the apartment I grew up in to one of EMI's floors. As we got out of the elevator we were met by Mike Schnapp like we were old friends. He led us through the offices, past all the cool posters and gold and platinum discs on the walls, to a big glass-walled conference room that had a view to die for. The room overlooked Manhattan and most of the city, exactly as I had envisioned it would on the subway ride uptown that morning. I had lived in New York City my entire life and this was the best view of the city I had ever seen. It was a clear day and you could see all the way to Kennedy Airport in one direction and the World Trade Center all the way downtown.

The three of us were sat on one side of the huge table, with Mike Schnapp and Davitt Sigerson opposite. Everyone at EMI was seemingly very excited to meet us. As we recounted our gig from the previous night, it was clear Davitt and Mike had made us an apparent priority.

'Gentlemen,' Davitt said, 'it's a pleasure to have you here to discuss your future, and how EMI could be a home for you and your music.' He was backlit by the huge floor-to-ceiling windows behind him, which made it all feel very cinematic. 'I have a great feeling about your band and, as I told you last night, Huey, I would like to make a record with you.'

I was having a moment, soaking it all in. The amazing view, the self-satisfaction of being in the big conference room discussing my future at EMI and the promise of what might be . . .

'Yeah, well, I think we should talk terms, you know, advances and royalties, Davitt . . .'

It was Jimmy. The guy just blurted out this dumb shit and blew the mood immediately. I turned to look at him and could tell he was over his skis. 'I think what Jimmy is trying to get to is important,' I was trying not to undermine Jimmy, but at the same time making Davitt and Mike understand there was a guy at the table who understood how things worked. I had no idea how things worked though; none. Even so, I felt that cutting to the chase and banging them about money right off the bat was lowering the tone of the meeting. 'The band are very excited to be able to make an album here potentially,' I continued, looking at Davitt as I spoke. 'I'm very excited to be here and I'm sure . . .' I turned to look at my side of the table now, where Steve was nodding but Jimmy was staring at me like he was being chastised. 'I'm sure we will be able to come to a mutually satisfying agreement about money. But, right now, I think we should talk about how EMI can help us get our music to the most ears as possible.'

That was all I could say without showing Davitt and Mike that Jimmy was talking shit, trying to sound like a big-time music manager. We went on to discuss, in detail, certain tunes that Davitt really liked. He thought that our song 'King of New York' had some elements that reminded him of Marvin Gaye's foray into blaxploitation soundtracks, with his groundbreaking album *Trouble Man*. We went full-muso and talked production techniques; Steve was the guy who wrote most of the music to 'King of New York', and told Davitt about how he got the inspiration for the sounds. I talked about how I was trying to tell stories that resonated with folks on more than one level, how I thought the band was truly original because of how we weaved live instrumentation with samples and fused rock, soul, funk and jazz thoughtfully.

Davitt got it. Considering he was the head of a major record label, he was a really cool guy. First and foremost, he was a music producer and, during the meeting, I learned to understand why the guys on the board of EMI Records had given him this big gig. We were all told that the music business was run by lawyers and accountants now, and it was quite refreshing to meet a guy who wasn't either.

As the conversation went on, Jimmy was all but relegated to the sidelines for the rest of the meeting. Unable to contribute about music, he sulked and made faces. He started to pout towards the end, and I felt that both Davitt and Mike were, along with me, wondering why he was there at all. We, as a band, didn't need a guy who had zero practical music business experience running his mouth about things he had very little understanding of. I didn't need his money anymore and it was becoming increasingly apparent I didn't need his street mentality poisoning this potential life-changing deal.

As the meeting wound up, we agreed to meet up the following week and start the process of negotiating a contract and signing a record deal. Steve and I were extremely excited. As we left the EMI offices we were in high spirits. But back on the street, Jimmy was immediately talking shit about the whole thing: 'They're trying to fuck you guys over with all the bullshit talk about how good your demo sounds. They want to low-ball the deal, I can tell. It's what I do to the dumb club kids who want to get over on me.'

Listening to him talk, I got the feeling that Jimmy knew he was out of his depth. Why else conflate dealing molly to club kids and a record contract? 'Bro, chill,' I replied. 'It was a great start. We were nowhere this time yesterday and now we have some fucking hope, you dumbass.'

At that Jimmy stopped walking. We were in Midtown Manhattan, it was a weekday and the sidewalks were full. As people flooded past us like a river, Jimmy and I stared at each other for a few moments. I could sense his animosity towards me, and I wasn't comfortable with it.

'Our potential record deal is not some grand scheme to fuck us all over. Yes, we must be careful as to how we proceed from here on out, but being stupid for no fucking reason other than your weed-induced paranoia is not fucking helping the situation.' Jimmy was giving me his best tough-guy look to no effect. I continued: 'As our manager your job is to not fuck things up because you can't scale up your thinking.' This last comment pissed him off as I had intended. I'm not an instigator by nature but I was getting to the point where I was questioning Jimmy's role and I felt that things might be better addressed head-on.

'Fuck you, Huey, you wise ass.' Jimmy was moving around like he was trying to work up the courage to take a pop at me. I clocked this and thought I had better put some distance between the two of us. I stepped back. 'Look at you, fuckin' pussy,' he sneered. 'You had better back the fuck up . . .'

I wasn't looking to fight him, but he was a dummy, and dummies do dumb shit. Jimmy was about six foot and a good 30 pounds heavier than I was. I wasn't scared of him, but I didn't want to make him my enemy. I saw the situation for what it was; Jimmy was embarrassed and this was his struggle session.

'Jimmy, we all want what's best for the band.' Steve had finally entered the conversation. 'I think Huey is just worried that you don't know a whole lot about the business side . . .' Steve was talking with his hands up in front of himself in an effort to de-escalate the situation.

'So now you think I don't know what I'm doing too?'

Jimmy waved his hand dismissively at both of us. Then he turned and said, 'Fuck y'all,' and stormed off in a huff.

The next time I went up to EMI to talk to Mike about stuff we needed to get straight before we did the deal, he said Davitt wanted a word with me. I was ushered into Davitt's office right before he left for the day. His office was a corner one with floor-to-ceiling views of New York City that must have inspired him on a daily basis. It was dusk and the lights of Manhattan were making themselves known in the surrounding valley of skyscrapers. Although we'd only met twice, he greeted me like an old friend. It sometimes seems that in the entertainment industry everyone is best friends and we all love each other, but with Davitt it felt oddly genuine.

'I'm glad we could talk a bit more privately,' Davitt said, showing me to a chair by a small black leather sofa at the window, which he dropped into with a sigh. 'It's really good to have this chance to get to know each other.'

I was a little wary of Davitt, not because he was showing signs I should have been wary of, but because of the power he held over what I wanted in my life. It was on a par with standing in front of my old commanding officer's commanding officer, with no idea why I was standing there in the first place. It all felt way above my pay grade.

'When I was a young man just getting into the business,'

Davitt began, offering me some sparkling water as he spoke, 'I had a boss who took the time to explain certain things to me.' As he spoke, I watched the city's lights coming on behind him. He had a way of making me feel settled in his imposing office, and I was confident that I wasn't being talked down to. 'When I speak to you I feel you are a young man who wants to understand more of what goes on around himself than he'd like to admit.' Davitt put his hands up. 'Don't get me wrong, we just met, but you give me the impression that you want to know as much as you can about this business, not just the music making side.'

He had summed me up and come to the conclusion that I was more than just a pretty face. It was hard not to feel flattered.

'Davitt, I've been dreaming of being right here for most of my life, the bad things I went through, the tough times . . .' I was getting a little emotional as I spoke. Davitt was nodding his head with his eyes closed in solidarity with my testimonial. '. . . They all led here. It's all good now that it meant I get to do this. And yes, man, I want to gain a working knowledge of this industry so I can make a life in it.'

'That is why I wanted to talk to you about your team today,' Davitt opened his eyes and looked at me down the barrel. 'Specifically your manager, James.'

I laughed gently at his calling 'Jimmy', 'James'. 'Yeah, it's just Jimmy, and, yeah, I hear ya.' I rubbed my mustache.

'He was a guy who helped us out with some cash when we needed it, and now that we're about to hit the big time,' I paused, pointed at Davitt and smiled my best De Niro smile. 'We need to whack him, right?'

Davitt's face froze, 'No, don't do that!'

'I'm kidding, D. Can I call you D?'

He was a little put out after my mob joke. 'No, it's Davitt, Huey.'

Ok, I took his point. I realized then that these music industry types were not to be included in my secret world of organized crime and violence. It was too foreign a concept for them to understand; using violence to solve a problem that might have been solved in another way.

'Sorry, Davitt,' I backtracked. 'I was fucking around. I know he's not the right guy. I'm trying to work a way he can get lost without it becoming too big a deal.'

Davitt nodded. 'I would like you to know that I, and EMI Records, really want to be the place where you call home. I fear, though, that if this . . . "Jimmy"?' He checked with me that he had said it right. I nodded, he continued.

'. . . I fear that if Jimmy continues in the role of manager of Fun Lovin' Criminals, that the home you may find, sadly won't be here at EMI.'

My face must have betrayed me because Davitt rushed to add, 'I want the best for you and the band, Huey, and for you and your band, I sincerely believe, that's signing a deal with us at EMI. I am just not confident that your present manager is equipped with the necessary tools to effectively manage your career going forwards.'

Davitt was making the case I had made to myself just a day before after my public bust up with Jimmy. I told Davitt I would talk to him and try to make him understand the position of the label. More importantly, I told Davitt that I would like to be the young man who could learn from someone willing to impart their knowledge. 'Davitt, I don't want to piss you off and make this deal go away. I'll get with the boys and then talk to Jimmy.' It was my turn to be defensive. 'Can you give me a day or two?'

Davitt was a little thrown by my apparent overreaction. 'Take as much time as you need,' he reassured. 'And if there is a catch anywhere along the way . . .'

I sighed. 'Oh, you mean money? I think he's realistic that if I pay him back what we owe him, that would be fair.'

Davitt was smiling now. 'In my experience, Huey, when there is a deal on the table, everyone wants to wet their beak.'

I laughed along with his bad mob joke. 'Yeah, you're right, that's something I hadn't factored in yet. Greed.'

We both nodded at the word.

'It's been good to talk today,' Davitt smiled. 'I'm glad to be working with you at the outset of your career. Remember that I'm here to talk about whatever you'd like to talk about concerning the process. Negotiating a record contract is something that requires good counsel. Do you have a lawyer yet?'

I hadn't thought of that yet. I mean, I knew I needed a lawyer, but right away?

'Have you heard of Clive Davis?' Davitt asked.

Clive Davis was a legend in the music business. He'd founded Arista Records and discovered numerous legendary musicians like Whitney Houston and Buster Rhymes.

'Yeah, I know that guy. I mean, not personally, you know . . .'

Davitt smiled patiently and continued, 'He's got a son, Fred Davis. He's a really good music lawyer and in a unique position to be a great deal of help in your near future.' He paused. 'I shouldn't really be helping you find an attorney who will be adversarial towards me in the near future, but he's your man. I will call him myself tomorrow morning to give him a heads-up.'

'Thanks, Davitt, I'll give him a call. And thanks for this . . .' I outstretched my hands, to show it was encompassing everything.

On my way downtown on the 2 train, I called Jimmy from a pay phone in the station and left a message, saying we needed to meet up.

Chapter Fourteen

Jimmy

'You know, I'm not some fucking punk you can scam outta money and not have it come back at you, Huey,' Jimmy spat, his Boston Celtics cap at a jaunty angle.

'That's not why I'm here,' I replied, because he was a volatile type of guy.

We were at his apartment in Midtown Manhattan and he was trying to save face by getting belligerent. I was sitting on his sofa while he was standing up by his big TV across from me in the mostly empty living room.

When Davitt told me that he and EMI weren't fully prepared to go further with us as a band if we kept Jimmy on as manager, it was down to me to give him 'the talk'. As with most things regarding business, the other guys in the band were happy to have me handle this type of shit.

It said everything about Jimmy that he had a huge Rottweiler dog named Shadow who liked me more than it did him. Jimmy had lent us some cash to print up our demos and paid Steve's brother some bread to mix it with us at his studio, but now that we had a potential deal brewing he was getting delusional. The word on the street was that he was a small-time drug dealer who had hit it big selling to the city's club dealers around the time molly got huge in the club scene.

I knew Jimmy's ego was going to lead the conversation so I let him tell me how much he did for me and how I was an ungrateful punk and so on. But when he told me about his .40 Glock I figured I might want some leverage of my own. 'I'm here because you know and I know this management thing you have with us isn't going to pan out . . .' I started.

At this revelation Jimmy turned and gave me his best Nino Brown act. 'You think you can do this without me? Fucking ungrateful bitch.'

I'm smart enough to know when someone is venting. All the same, I told Jimmy that talking reckless was one thing, but if he was to try to get tough with that Glock of his I wasn't going to roll over like the aforementioned 'bitch': 'Bro, I respect your position and I am grateful for what you've done for me.' I sat forwards now. 'But street shit like this isn't going to cut it uptown at EMI. You saw how they played you off at the meeting.' Jimmy lowered his eyes from mine and looked out of the window. I rolled it up for him politely. 'They want someone to manage us who has done this kind of thing at this high level before. You just ain't that guy, Jimmy.'

'Fuck you!' he shouted and made a hesitant move towards me. His Rottweiler gave a low growl in response to his indecision. I stood up from the leather sofa and got ready. Jimmy was so mad that he was looking around for something to hit me with. He was bigger than me, but it was all fat.

Cooler heads eventually prevailed after some heated disagreement. It didn't come to violence, but it was real fucking close. I left with the understanding that he and I were not good anymore and I was now his enemy. That didn't bother me as much as his supposed claim to be 'our manager'. We didn't have a contract because it was a street thing, and when street things don't work out, where I come from it ends one of two ways: silver or lead.

Because I had never asked my 'in-laws' downtown for money or, really, anything for marrying Isabella, I had a very easy relationship with a few guys from the outfit that my 'in-laws' were affiliated with. They were initially suspicious of my fidelity but eventually realized I was authentic in my intentions. After the meeting with Jimmy, I went downtown to Little Italy and visited with a friend of mine named Joey Pips. Joey told me to just mention his name to Jimmy if he had any more questions as to why I was taking the band in a new direction: 'Just tell him my name, cuz, and to ask around about me. Everybody knows me . . .' Joey was a younger generation guy who had been made recently. He was more than ready to flex the muscle that being a made guy comes with. Joey was old school like that: he preferred fear over love when it came to his reputation. He embraced the mob guy aesthetic with abandon. He was the type to wear double-knit trousers like he was in the movie *Goodfellas* and spoke with both his index and pinky fingers at the same time. 'The fuck will be shining your fucking shoes by sundown. *Quel fottuto tizio non ha idea di come potrebbe farsi male essendo così stupido.*'

'Joey, I don't speak Italian,' I laughed. He was hilarious but also very violent, so I chose my words carefully. 'Is the "*stupido*" about him?' I asked. 'Yeah, he's stupid. I don't think he's smart enough to be scared, and that's no reflection on you, he's just simple in the head.'

I didn't think some ecstasy dealer would care that I was 'connected' either. But I was also thinking, if I did actually drop my friend's name, what would happen then? Would Jimmy tell me to go fuck myself and shoot me? Would Joey now be in charge of my destiny for my accepting his help? What would be the trade-off to get rid of the Jimmy problem? Would it be another equally complicated problem but this time involving the mafia?

I weighed this all up in my head. In the end, I took the approach that would best serve the situation and keep me out of anyone's clutches moving forwards. I met up again with

Jimmy at his empty apartment that smelled of stale weed. I told him that I was going to pay him back all the money he'd lent us and something significant enough on top of that to keep him humble. 'I don't want any bad blood here, or you thinking I'm trying to fuck you over.' I put a manila envelope on his coffee table. 'There's a couple grand more in there to keep your manners intact.'

Jimmy picked up the envelope and opened it enough for him to see the money inside. I had gotten few Gs from Angie to cover the buyout. He was still pissed off at me and the situation but seemed to have realized in the interim that I was not some chump off the street. I would give him a fight if he wanted one, and he didn't really want one.

I continued with my proposal, but put an edge on my voice now. 'I gotta tell you, bro, I'm not the type to get all mushy when some out-of-shape motherfucker waves a gun around. If you try that tough-guy shit again with me . . .'

I've been told that when I want to be, I can be the weather.

'. . . I'll kill you.'

He blinked.

That was that. Silver or lead, just like in the movies.

When we all next convened at EMI I had streamlined the Fun Lovin' Criminals to everyone's delight.

Chapter Fifteen

My New Best Friend

'**M**ike, you fuckin' pimp!'

Mike Schnapp was one of the coolest, nicest cats I had ever met. In the early stages of our courtship with EMI Records, I spent most days with him, and he quickly became my new best friend. Mike was living his best rock and roll life and was happy to take me along for the ride. EMI had given him an extraordinarily huge expense account when he signed on as their new vice president of A&R and Mike dutifully beat the shit out of it every chance he could get.

When Mike first offered to pick me up, I wondered what sort of car an A&R guy drove. The answer, a 1976 Cadillac Eldorado, was less an automobile and more a yacht that Mike captained around the city. Dark burgundy red with a white convertible top and white leather interior, it was easily 18 feet long, with two huge sofas as the interior. While the vehicle was beautiful, it was also not in pristine shape. Mike parked it on the streets of New York and that takes a toll on any car. Even so, I loved it at first sight.

'Jump in, Huey! We're going to get in some trouble!' Mike shouted in his distinctive tones as he pulled over to pick me up.

'Hey, man, so where's the trouble?' I asked as Mike slid the glossy red battleship away from the curb and guided it through the Manhattan traffic.

'Downtown. I know a few people at a place called Max Fish.'

Shit!, I thought to myself. That wasn't the sort of trouble Mike was probably thinking of. Max Fish was down on Ludlow Street where I used to live, where that girl OD'd. Not that he or anybody else knew as I kept all that to myself. 'Cool,' I said, attempting and failing to be.

'You ok, man?' Mike could tell something was off, he had a good radar for that.

I tried to play it off but didn't do a good job. 'Yeah, I just have some history on the block . . .' I trailed off.

Mike turned to look at me. 'Are you in trouble down there?'

'Nothing like that, just some bad memories.' I lit a smoke and Mike hit the button for my window to slide open. Turned out I was the only person Mike let smoke in his car, though he did insist on the window, or the top, being down.

'Maybe we should go somewhere else then. I'm cool . . .'

I realized this guy was a solid friend, of which I didn't have many.

'No, Mike, let's do it.' I was determined not to be a bummer. 'We can make some new memories, right?'

Mike smiled and replied in kind. 'Right you are!'

When we got to the Lower East Side every traffic-light stop involved somebody telling Mike how fly his car was, which he took in his stride. Mike had a cool way about him: he was old school in most of his social skills, and had a great sense of humour about life and himself (being able to laugh at yourself is one of life's superpowers). The two types of people who had the best comments as we pulled up were either old Jewish guys who told us of how they used to have what Mike called a 'Jew canoe' back in the day. (Mike was Jewish, so he could say that.) The other type was the Latino. *Mi gente!*

As Mike put it when we took the right-hand turn onto Ludlow Street right past Katz's Deli on the corner, 'My Latino brothers were the guys who bought the canoe from the Jew when he moved out to Five Towns.'

It was almost lyrical the way Mike distilled it for me. I was kind of nervous being back on the block, but I held it down as best I could as we pulled up.

'Hey, excuse me, my man!' Mike was shouting at some dude smoking by the curb by the door to the hipster bar, Max Fish. The guy got the hint and moved back onto the sidewalk as Mike docked the huge automobile. When the smoke cleared and the car was parked up by the door, I could see inside the bar as far as the surreal Julio Iglesias photo where he looked like his face was sliding off his skull. If you know, you know.

'Mike Schnapp! Our brother in Christ!' Out of the bar came a guy with long blond hair and a beanie. He walked up to the Caddy, giving Mike the handshake and hug combo awkwardly through the car's open window. Then he saw me in the passenger seat. 'Hey, man, any friend of Mike's . . .' he paused and looked back and forth between me and Mike. 'Well, you know . . .' he trailed off, dissing his joke without telling us the punchline. 'I'm Carlo,' he said as he took the joint from Mike and stood up to smoke it.

Mike, I noticed, had put the car into park but hadn't turned it off. Mike, I noticed, had noticed me noticing. Always be ready.

'This is my friend Huey,' Mike offered to Carlo.

I put my hand out for a shake and got a solid one back.

'Huey, good to meet you, what do you drink?'

Mike saw me look confusingly back at Carlo. 'Carlo is the manager of the joint,' he explained.

'Oh, shit, yeah, man, sorry,' I took the joint from Carlo's hand and puffed it. 'Any beer that's cold, thank you, bro.'

Carlo nodded and sauntered back into the blurry bar past the sidewalk full of loitering hipsters.

'Carlo is a good bro, his best friend is the music writer Steve Blush.' Mike snapped his fingers, trying to remember something he had forgotten. 'He makes a special effort when I come downtown.'

'Fuck yeah he does,' I laughed. 'I wouldn't be surprised if he came back on roller skates with a few burgers and fries . . .'

Mike grabbed an 8-track cassette tape from the glove compartment and looked it over. '*Zeppelin II*?' he asked, holding the big piece of plastic up for me to see.

By now Carlo was coming back through the throng of people milling around in front of Max Fish with our drinks on a tray. As he picked his way through, saying hello to folks along the way, I tried to take in the moment. This, I realized, was the beginning of a new era of my life. I wasn't some lowly street guy pulling some kind of slick move, no. I was . . . transcending. 'Yeah, that's a good one, Mike,' I said as Carlo passed me a Rolling Rock across the wide front seat.

'*Chela*,' Carlo said to me as 'Whole Lotta Love' began its magic in earnest. Mike's superb old-school stereo had some decent sound considering it was from 1976.

'Damn, Mike, shit is bumpin',' I yelled over Robert Plant's moaning during the long breakdown. I took a big swig on possibly the best tasting beer I'd ever had. It was ice cold, just the way I liked it.

Mike pointed to the dashboard, specifically to the bottom

of it. I could make out some lights from an aftermarket power amp. 'I had that installed when I got it. I am in the music biz, ya know?' he said as way of an explanation.

'Gents,' Carlo took this moment to bid us farewell, 'I've got things to see and people to . . .' he paused, the joke withering on the vine just like before. It didn't matter, though, because I had just been served a beer from a bar in a car at the curb.

Life was looking up.

The visit to Max Fish was just the beginning. We would cruise around blazing joints in the Caddy, stopping here and there for a drink and whatnot. When we went downtown, it was an absolute revelation. I thought I knew a lot of people in Manhattan, but Mike seemed to know everybody who was worth knowing. They all loved Mike and, as his new protégé, I started getting some residual love as well.

Mike introduced me to a whole new New York scene, where people were genuinely interested in me and my band. These cats and kittens were the real NYC rock crowd that Mike came up with during the heyday of the eighties' metal scene. He'd started in the music business as a promotions guy at a smallish metal label and worked his way up to the majors. There he landed at Epic Records where he worked with bands like Pearl Jam, Alice in Chains, Rage Against the Machine and Ozzy Osbourne. Ozzy's wife and manager,

Sharon Osbourne, saw the awesomeness in Mike when he worked on Ozzy's solo career and made sure everyone knew how valuable he was to Ozzy's success, which got Mike the attention he deserved. He was a real stand-up guy who did what he said, stood up for his artists and made clear he was their guy. Apparently he threatened other record company A&R guys to stay away from Fun Lovin' Criminals during this period, making clear we were HIS band.

Mike knew I had quit my job at the clubs and was pretty broke, so he sometimes bought me cigarettes in addition to smoking me up and feeding me. We would go out to dinner most evenings and lunch most days when I came by the office. We both really loved the Palm steak restaurant on 2nd Avenue right near the UN. I was crazy skinny, 140 pounds dipped in water and 20 pounds lighter than in the Marines, so I sure didn't mind the new nutrition Mike was providing. We would go on 'pizza tours' around New York City every weekend, hitting up five or six different pizza joints and grabbing a slice at each to judge which was the best.

All this food wasn't the only sustenance Mike was giving me. Over these very nice dinners, he explained all the things I needed to know to make educated decisions regarding the music business. Mike would tell me, confidentially, things that would help me understand what the label was prepared to do and what they weren't. Through this information I managed to get a 'cost of living' advance from Davitt to tide me and the boys over until the record deal got done and some money was coming in.

It was great to have a personal guide to the music business, but even better to have a new homie with a fly Caddy and some clout who liked to dine out. Mike was closer to my age than the two other Fun Lovin' Criminals guys. We bonded through our love of the same music and similar upbringings. We both were fans of all that classic rock we were fed on FM radio in the New York area in the 1970s: Zep, Neil Young, Yes and Sabbath were all entries in Mike's 8-track cassette collection.

Mike comes from the Five Towns part of Long Island. Sometimes we'd drive out to Long Beach in the Caddy smoking joints with the top down. Mike used to live out that way we'd take my dog Sugar for walks on the beach when it was deserted and really beautiful. We would hit up seafood places like Bigelow's New England Fried Clams house near Massapequa for lunch and the world famous All American Burger on the way back into the city.

Mike had an ethos he used day to day. *Whatever it takes.* He would do 'whatever it takes' to get the job done and make his musicians happy. None of the musicians he'd worked with ever forgot that.

One time I was hanging out with Mike at a rock show downtown when he saw Vernon Reid, the guitarist in Living Colour. I was in awe: Vernon is one of my favourite musicians and the stuff he did with the band The Decoding Society is hugely impressive. As Vernon made his way through the crowd, Mike called out to him. Vernon's reaction to seeing Mike was like every other time a famous rock musician spotted Mike; they were genuinely delighted to see him. 'Mike Schnapp! My man!' Vernon shouted in response.

'Vernon, this is my friend Huey, I'm about to sign his band Fun Lovin' Criminals to EMI.'

I was beaming. Mike was introducing me to one of my heroes. 'Hey, Vernon, big fan of yours.' I tried to stay cool as we shook hands. Vernon cut a dashing figure in the dark, his short dreads poking up out of his hat, and his silver rings catching the flashing light.

'You're in good company with Mike,' Vernon told me. 'He's a stand-up guy . . . a mensch, right?' Vernon looked over at Mike, who nodded his approval. Then he turned his attention back to me. 'Have you recorded the album yet? Bro,' he motioned to Mike, 'said you are "about" to sign.'

'Not yet man, can't wait though.' I smiled like a dummy.

'You are about to go on a big adventure, man,' Vernon raised his arms to emphasize his point. 'The adventure of a lifetime.' He leaned in. 'You want some free advice, Huey?'

I couldn't believe it; Vernon Reid was dropping some science on me.

'Yeah, sure, Vernon, thank you, I'm all ears.' I was

speaking too quickly for my liking, unable to hide the fact I was star-struck.

Vernon, thankfully, didn't act like he noticed. 'The first thing you need to learn is to enjoy the ride, my man,' he told me. 'It's not a long ride most of the time, but it's a crazy ride that very few people on God's earth ever get to take. It's as magical as you let it become, but you gotta remember, bro . . . you're never the man for long.'

With that, Vernon smiled, turned back to Mike and gave him a warm hug. Then he disappeared back into the smoky recesses of the dark nightclub.

'You're never the man for long,' I repeated to myself, willing it into my brain as Vernon left.

An ethos to live by? Why not?

One rainy afternoon Mike called me up on my tiny cell phone, which I was an early proponent of, and asked if I wanted to go see Motörhead play an intimate gig in the village that evening.

'Man, I fucking love Motörhead,' I told Mike excitedly.

For me, the type of down and dirty heavy rock music the band created was truly singular. The lead vocalist and bass player, Lemmy Kilmister, was a rock and roll legend and – guess what? – a personal friend of Mike's too. Mike told me we were on the guestlist and if we got there early enough we might get a chance to meet the man himself. I made sure we were there in plenty of time.

Motörhead were playing some sort of corporate gig on Bleecker Street in the West Village at a venue that held less than three hundred people. Mike picked me up in the Caddy and we arrived with an hour to spare, smoking a joint while deciding what to do next; the rain was coming down and the queue to get in was pretty long. So we hung in the car, hot boxing it with weed smoke, waiting until we saw a break in the line. I was getting really excited and Mike could tell I was psyched. 'If you introduce me to Lemmy, shit, Mike . . . Lemmy!' I made the 'metal' sign with my hand and Mike nodded in agreement.

When we finally got out of the car, the line of rock fans waiting in the rain smelled us before they saw us. The blue weed smoke billowed out of the open doors enveloping the sidewalk and all that traversed it. Mike passed me the joint over the top of the Caddy's white soft top and I looked around taking in the scene. There were a few people still on line, waiting to get in and the usual bustle of Bleecker Street foot traffic kept it moving as we walked to the front of the queue, finishing up the joint.

'Hello, my man!' Mike boomed to the security dude and some lady with a clipboard. 'We are on the band's list. I'm Mike Schnapp and this is my friend Huey, no last name . . .'

I loved that Mike was going along with my unusual

insistence of forgoing the use of surnames. Where I came from, we didn't care, need or even want to know your last name. Last names come with inherent problems like history, heritage and having to remember them.

As we were led into the club, I noticed and appreciated how Mike operated. He might have been a big gregarious guy but he was also extremely polite to people. That politeness alloyed with authenticity made him a charismatic force of nature. Despite never having been in the club before, he knew exactly where the backstage entrance was. Standing there was an English guy who looked like an extra from some B-movie version of *Sinbad*. Unsurprisingly, he knew exactly who Mike was. 'Mike Schnapp, you old sod!' Hugs were given and received. I even got one from the pirate after Mike had done the introductions. Mike was like a proud big brother, and I found that really cool. I had been an only child growing up and the idea of brotherhood was something I had only learned later in the service, appreciating it all the more.

'Huey's in a band I'm signing,' Mike explained. 'He's one hell of a guitar player and I think Lemmy would like to meet him.'

The pirate checked his watch. 'Sure, there's still an hour to the gig. Lemmy's back in his dressing room, so I'll check he's not with some bird and tell him you're here . . .'

He disappeared backstage and Mike turned to me and

smiled. 'I forgot that guy's name, but he's been with Lemmy forever.'

I lit a cigarette and took in the small club. There were the typical old-school Motörhead fans, if that was even a thing; older bottle blondes with some miles on them with their Long Island metal dude boyfriends, their long hair having to be cut short for work. My favourites were the lovely newbies to the Motörhead universe: young rock chicks who had daddy issues and bad taste in tattoos. There was a smattering of rock press Mike was on nodding terms with, and the pretentious NYC metal tastemakers who acted like they were the ones who were famous.

Before too long Riki Rachtman rolled up on us. Riki hosted an MTV show called *Headbanger's Ball*, which was the epitome of rock cool when it came the heavy metal television in the USA. The show broke new acts and even had the power to revive older ones. Mike, of course, was good friends with this cat. From what I could gather during the short conversation happening in front of me, Mike had been once again very helpful to Riki and the show somehow.

'Have you seen Lemmy yet?' Riki asked Mike.

'No, my man, just got here with Huey,' Mike smiled.

Riki gave me a nod and then looked around. He seemed cool to me, just too self-conscious. Being on TV does that to people if they don't watch out. 'He's in a good mood,' Riki turned back to Mike. 'But he's drinkin' . . .' The pair pulled knowing faces. Then Riki gave Mike a pound, me another 'cool' nod, turned and hit the bar on the far side of the room.

At this moment the pirate returned, opening the back-stage door we'd been dutifully standing in front of, and whisking us through, where were handed Motörhead AAA passes. 'Lemmy's in the last room on the left,' the pirate pointed.

The room in question was easy enough to find, given it had 'Lemmy' stencilled on it like an ammunition bunker. We got there just as a woman was leaving. She paid us no mind and rushed past, leaving the door ajar. Mike got to it first and looked inside. 'Hello? Lemmy? My man?' For the first time since I'd known him, Mike sounded a little nervous.

From the other side of the door rumbled a familiar voice I had heard countless times before. This was the voice who warned me of the dangers of gambling in his infamous song 'Ace of Spades', the voice who told us all of the pleasures of travelling to South America in his jaunty tune, 'Going to Brazil'. It was none other than the bona fide legend of rock and roll . . . 'Mike, you sight for sore eyes!' Lemmy came into my view from the doorway and embraced Mike like they were long lost brothers.

'Lemmy, my man! It's great to see you again.' Mike ushered me into the dressing room. 'This is my friend Huey. I'm just signing his band to EMI. He's a huge fan.'

I was blushing. Lemmy was just so cool. He was wearing

black jeans, embroidered monochromatic leather cowboy boots, a black t-shirt with cut sleeves and some kind of German military cap askew. 'Hey, man, it's really nice to meet you,' I said, putting out my hand.

As Lemmy took it in a solid grip, he looked into my eyes like he was looking into my soul. 'Mike is the real fucking deal, mate,' he said, all serious. 'I know this man well and have seen the power he can summon.' Lemmy glanced over to Mike, now unable to keep the straight face he'd been trying on me. His face cracked into a smile. 'If he's vouching for you like this, son, you must be the man of the moment,' Lemmy laughed.

We all had a laugh at my uncomfortable 'moment'. Then Lemmy asked me if I wanted a drink.

'Sure, man.' How could you refuse a drink from Lemmy? 'Whatever you're having . . .' The second I finished speaking I knew I had fucked up. There are myriad stories about how Lemmy liked to drink to excess. So much so that he was more likely to have a bottle of bourbon in his hand than his famous Rickenbacker bass guitar. Lemmy pulled two water glasses from a side table and a bottle of amber liquor. He sat down at the table in the centre of the room and grinned. Mike stayed standing, knowing better than to sit down. I sat down across from Lemmy, smiling like a dummy who didn't know how cooked he actually was.

I watched as Lemmy poured the amber liquor from the

bottle into the first glass, filling it up to almost the top. He paused to smile at me and then poured the same amount into the other glass. He held up one of the glasses, in a toast, and asked me a question. 'Huey, you want to be a rock and roll star?'

'Yeah, I guess,' I blurted. 'I mean, I've been playing music most of my life and I would like to . . .' Lemmy gave me a look that told me he was unconvinced, so I stammered on, more convincingly now. 'Shit! Yes, Lemmy, I would!' I grabbed the other glass filled with liquor and met Lemmy's eye. I'm sure he saw the fire in my own, giving me a look back with some of his own thrown in for good measure.

'Good man,' he winked.

At that I slugged the whole damn glass downed in one go. I didn't bother to see what Lemmy did. I wanted to be a rock and roll star. I knew what I was supposed to do, damnit.

Wow! I wasn't sure what I had just downed, but that liquor had some kick. For a moment, I thought I was going to throw it all back up onto Lemmy's cool boots. Fortunately, my military bearing and an imagined life of ridicule if I did fortified me not to. By the time my eyes stopped watering and I could finally see across the table again Lemmy had put his glass back down on it. I noticed it was just a little drained from the modest sip he had taken.

Mike and Lemmy were guffawing away at me and my earnest attempt to be 'rock and roll'. As they started to jostle me around and make it clear it was all in good fun, I joined in the laughter. I must have passed the test because when we all calmed down Lemmy put his hand on my shoulder and said to Mike, 'He's going to be just fine.' Then he turned to me, smiling warmly, 'Right, kid?'

I was drunk as fuck and Lemmy Kilmister just told me I was part of the club.

'Yeah, I got this. Thank you, man.' I gave him a drunken hug and turned to leave him in peace. Over my shoulder, I heard him say to Mike, 'Marines are fuckin' crazy. Enjoy the show . . .'

When we were out of the backstage area I apologized to Mike for getting drunk around Lemmy and acting silly. But Mike just laughed and told me that I was crazy for thinking that I was out of line. 'If Lemmy was pissed off, we would not be unsure of that fact,' Mike grinned. 'I think he liked you.'

I was relieved. I started smiling to myself remembering how I tried to out-drink Lemmy in his own dressing room. 'Yeah, he looked surprised as hell when I downed the whole glass.'

Mike was smiling like my approving big brother, 'We both were Huey, we both were.'

After the gig, Mike and I tried to go backstage again to thank Lemmy for his hospitality. But old and new friends or not, the pirate wouldn't let us through. A few of those rock chicks with daddy issues and bad tattoos had beaten us to it.

Chapter Sixteen

Epiphany

'It's a weird time to be me, Gino.'

I was sitting at the bar in an infamous spaghetti joint down in Little Italy waiting for a latecomer. The latecomer was a delivery guy who had a package for me to take to Angie. Who knew when he would show, and so Gino had pulled up a stool and given me a beer while I waited.

'Where are you at with everything?' Gino asked. 'I thought you were the big rock star now?'

'Not quite yet,' I smiled. 'I'm finished negotiating the record deal; we did great on that.' The beer I was drinking was greasing my gears and Gino, who I met there whenever I did errands for Angie downtown, was gonna get an earful. 'Now the heavy lift is the publishing deal,' I explained, putting my beer back on the bar.

Gino was tall dark and ugly. The pockmarks on his cheeks weren't as bad as his wide set eyes and 'goober mouth'. He was very smart, though, and despite only being 30 was one of the local wise-guy restaurant managers who knew the score when it came to who was who in the neighbourhood. He was leaning on the bar next to me while a zip (a guy just off the boat from Italy, who knew 'zip') who was cleaning up kept us comfortable with drinks and nibbles. Gino was sipping at what looked like a mint julep. 'So publishing is different from a recording deal? How?' he asked.

'All bands who put out a record have to register the songs on that record and who wrote them.'

Gino nodded along while the zip looked from me to Gino like it was a tennis match; he was probably just trying to keep up.

'When the song is broadcast on radio or used in a film or on TV,' I kept going, 'the people responsible for the writing of the song have to get compensated. The task of registering and collecting that revenue for the song is usually relegated to a publishing company.'

As I was explaining this to Gino I got the distinct feeling of being watched, and not just by the zip. I glanced around but didn't see anyone I knew. From the bar I had a full view of the main restaurant except for the private room at the back. There had been a big table in there that had let out a few minutes after I had gotten here. Their nice long two-hour lunch left a few stragglers in the rear room but I couldn't see clearly back there.

Gino saw me checking the place out and teased me. 'You see any Viet Cong, Marine?'

I popped back into the conversation, shaking my head. 'No, dumbass. The deal I'm cutting now is with a publishing company who will get me and my band the money we're due when we sell our album.'

The zip got his name called from the kitchen, apologized and then ran off without another word. Gino gave me the look like I should continue, so I did.

'The company is giving us an advance on this possible future income. My lawyer, Fred, who up until just a few months ago actually fucking worked at EMI as their head of A&R, got us a tremendous royalty rate on record sales and a bunch of backend money for producing it.'

Gino was intrigued, but now it was his turn to scan the restaurant. The latecomer had just arrived, so he gave me the 'wrap-it-up' hand gesture.

'Fred's father is Clive Davis.' I waited for Gino to recognize the name I had just dropped, but he didn't know shit from a shingle. 'Clive Davis is a music business legend, started Arista Records. He discovered Springsteen, Pink Floyd . . .'

Gino jumped in then. 'I love Floyd, saw the laser thing at the planetarium last month – epic!'

I nodded at this and continued. 'Yeah, well, the new head A&R guy, Brian Koppelman, was the son of one of the guys on the EMI board of directors and this guy on the board, Charles Koppelman, was a rival of Fred's dad Clive.' I was trying to paint a picture but I had run out of paint. And time. 'Long story short,' I eyed the courier walking out of the kitchen where the office was. 'Fred had known what the label could actually do because he had just been working there. And he played them right up to the limit. Every time the head of the label gave in to his – I mean, our – demands—'

Another wise guy we will call Paul came out from the kitchen at that moment with a backpack in his arms holding it flat like a pizza. That was what I was waiting for. I finished my beer and got up from the bar. Gino stood up too, giving me a small hug as a goodbye. 'Sounds like you've got a good lawyer there, Huey.'

'Yeah I do, the publishing advance is the icing on the cake.'

As I walked outside Gino followed me to the curb where Mateo was waiting in his VW Jetta.

'Good luck with all that music stuff, Huey. We are all rooting for you.'

That was a really nice thing for Gino to say. I knew Angie had bragged to a few guys downtown about my record deal, and it was cool to hear they were supportive. Angie had beat the RICO thing but she was still keeping things very low-key, hence why I was doing these errands again. As I opened up the door of the car to get in, Mateo saw Gino and asked from the driver's seat, 'What are your specials today, big G?'

Gino didn't even blink. 'Hello, Mateo.' He rolled his eyes at me and Mateo and laughed. 'Are you two guys always hungry?'

A few days later, I headed over to Fred Davis's office on West 57th Street for an after-lunch meeting. As I got to his office building, Fred was just closing a taxi's door by the curb. He looked in a good mood and gave me a hearty handshake in greeting: 'Good to see you, Huey. Looking sharp.'

I checked my reflection in the glass all over the large garish lobby and took it as a compliment. I was still having trouble getting more than four hours of sleep and I tended to take stuff personally when I was tired.

'Thank you, Fred,' I managed, trying to not talk too much as we reached the elevators in the lobby. In my experience it shows low moral character to blather in front of strangers while waiting for an elevator. It was reassuring to see Fred shared my reticence as he mumbled a reply. I made some low guttural sound in agreement and we stayed silent until we entered his law offices. We said hello to his assistant so as to not seem unpleasant, but everyone else got the cold shoulder until we had our relative privacy.

Fred had a swanky office that took up half a floor of the

building. He offered me a chair opposite his desk and I took it, studying the art behind his head on the wall. I was focusing on that because Fred had recently gotten what looked to me like a hair transplant. It wasn't my business as to why he got one, and I kept my questions and reservations to myself. I also didn't want to seem unkind by staring at his head and then ignoring what was sat upon it. I figured I didn't have to ignore something I failed to acknowledge.

Fred, by contrast, was keen to acknowledge what he'd seen before. 'So, Huey. This might sound an odd question but did you by any chance have lunch at a certain spaghetti joint in Little Italy last Friday?' He winked like he caught me doing something wrong. 'I could absolutely swear to God that I saw you there . . .'

'Oh, yeah?' Funny, I thought. I didn't remember going out for lunch that day. But then it clicked. I remembered the drink with Gino, sitting in the bar while waiting for the latecomer to appear with his delivery.

Fred sat forwards in his chair. 'You know that is a place where some rough people hang out?'

Why are you telling me something I obviously know? I wondered. Was he just being a caring guy, looking out for me? Another thought popped into my head: forget about what *I* was doing, why the fuck was he having lunch at a notorious mafia hangout?

As my brain was processing all this, I decided to ask him

something. 'Hey, is anything I tell you covered by attorney–client confidentiality?'

It took a second for Fred to register what I had just asked. But when it did, he sat back and laughed. 'Yeah, it is.'

Then the smile vanished. Fred made a serious face, then got up from his desk and walked over to the office door. Looking around, he quietly closed the door with a click. As he walked back towards his desk, he said softly behind me, 'I can't fucking wait to hear this.'

I told him everything. It took almost an hour.

Once I started, I couldn't stop. I hadn't told anyone everything before but here I was baring my soul to him. The homeless stuff. Angie and her stuff. I even told him about my mental health struggles and how I was just barely managing to balance it all. Fred heard everything like he was my confessor; he didn't try to interrupt or ask for clarifications, but just let me talk.

After I had finished, Fred took a moment to review what I had just told him. He'd been poker-faced during my explanation and in no hurry to give away what he thought. I was a little nervous as I sat there waiting for him to respond. Had I said too much? Could I trust him? I watched as he moved his desk phone away from his right arm with a withering stare, making sure no lights were lit on it. At that point, I realized I wasn't the only nervous person in the room.

'Listen,' he said. 'I know how this thing works, Huey.

Well, maybe not as well as you do . . .' Although we hadn't known each other long, we had a pretty good rapport. When he knew he was at the end of his knowledge he always admitted it. To me that showed good character. He continued speaking in that same spirit. 'But I have to ask. Is there a danger of these two worlds colliding?' He was holding his two hands up in front of himself, palms up. He didn't need to slam his hands together for me to know what he meant.

I understood Fred's reticence at my nonchalant attitude but I also knew I had to lay out everything without a filter. That's why I had asked him if I was covered, so he couldn't rat me out if push came to court. I reminded him he'd said I was covered before I continued. 'With all that I've told you, you can see why I was there at the restaurant. You can also understand why it's hard for me to share this with EMI, or the guys in my band. What do you think I should do?'

From his pause, I could feel that Fred was choosing his words with care. 'Huey, as your attorney, I can say that you're walking a very fine line when it comes to your in-laws. I would like to see you have less to do with them, of course. You are a recording artist now.' He paused again, so this particular comment had time to land.

Which it did, like a brick.

'You have a very bright future,' Fred continued. 'And your ongoing participation in a criminal enterprise is, frankly, counterintuitive.' He finished by giving me a look to add that he knew I wasn't stupid, so I shouldn't take it that way. I hadn't taken it that way, but I still didn't say anything more.

'Hmm?' He added when he saw me thinking.

I brought myself back into the room. 'Yeah, I know,' I replied.

As important as the mafia issue was, I was more concerned with the personal stuff I had divulged as well. 'What about my mind, Fred?' I asked him point blank. It was a simple question, but from his reluctance to answer, maybe a lawyer wasn't the person I should have been asking about it.

'Huey, I'm your lawyer . . . and I'm also a friend . . .' His uncomfortableness with the way I was so open about my struggles with depression and stuff was not uncommon. 'But I think . . .' Fred stopped to think about what he was going to say next, which made me pay even closer attention. 'I'm really not the best person you should be talking about the personal stuff with. Don't get me wrong, I've got a lot of time for you, son . . .'

By now I could see Fred was doing his best to be nice, and I was beginning to feel very embarrassed for over-sharing. Fred recognized that and gently said, 'Huey, do you have a shrink? You know, someone who you can talk to about things like this?'

At that I realized I had indeed been barking up the wrong tree. I laughed a little to cover my embarrassment. 'I do. I'm sorry, man . . . It all just kind of comes out together, like a band of gypsies.'

I stood up, feeling the need to move. 'You're a good dude Fred, thanks for letting me vent.' I was avoiding his eye as I put on my leather jacket. I had the need for some fresh air, to get out of there.

As I opened the door of his office, Fred called after me. 'Just take it slow, Huey.' I looked back at him as he continued. 'We'll get there. Don't worry about the business stuff as much as you are.' He stood up and came to meet me by the door. I had paused when he spoke to be polite, hearing him out. But I was not listening anymore. I knew who I needed to speak to.

Fred offered me his hand. 'I'll take care of stuff here, uptown.'

I looked at him. I could see he was making an effort to be folksy. There was a twinkle in my eye that was hard to resist. 'Thanks, Fred.' So I took his hand and felt the warmth in his shake. 'And I'll take care of stuff downtown . . .' I had made a decision at that moment to follow my heart, my brain and my lawyer. It was high time I told Angie she needed to find another errand boy, this man had some opportunities to take.

Outside Fred's office, another yellow taxi was idling in the same spot where I'd met Fred earlier. I called Joyce, who answered straightaway. 'Hello, Huey. Are you ok?'

'Yeah, I'm fine.' I realized Joyce was worried by my call so I tried to reassure her. 'I'm uptown at my lawyer's office and I've just had an epiphany,' I blurted out.

What a crazy thing to say, I thought to myself. Joyce must think I was nuts with these wacky lyrics.

Instead, I thought I heard her chuckle. 'Really? Epiphanies are good.' Immediately I relaxed. Joyce was such a kind woman. I could tell from her tone she was genuinely interested in me. 'I had a fleeting moment of clarity,' I explained, 'and I think it was kind of jarring for my lawyer to witness it.'

Joyce laughed. 'I'm at my apartment grading papers.' I could almost see her check her stainless-steel Omega Moon watch she always wore. 'I can see you in about an hour, if that is convenient?'

Joyce had an amazing penthouse apartment on 6th Avenue and 13th Street that overlooked all of Greenwich Village and the East Side, all the way to the East River. It was a grand place that was big enough for her to have another office there. This one had a view of the Con Edison power plant on 14th Street, and stretched all the way south to the Williamsburg Bridge.

Joyce also had a boyfriend who was considerably younger than she was. He was cool with me when he answered the door. 'Hey, man.' The boyfriend was about 35 and reminded me of Bob Weir from the Grateful Dead. Without doing the math I thought Joyce had 20 years on him, easy. No big deal, I thought. Love is love and anyone who gets a taste of it knows it to be a very special and fleeting part of life. 'Joyce is in her inner sanctum.' Her boyfriend led me down a hallway with that great view of the city on one side and a series of very beautiful framed Japanese illustrations of feudal life on the other.

The office door opened and Joyce welcomed me in with a smile and a, 'Hello there, Huey.'

'Hey, Joyce,' I crooned. I heard the door close shut quietly behind me and while I gave Joyce her customary two-kiss greeting, she gently guided me to a sofa with some flower patterns on it.

'This epiphany, my boy, tell me more,' she asked as she sat next to me.

'I was having a meeting about some publishing stuff,' I explained, 'and this guy I'm working with, Fred, says he saw me hanging around this spot downtown where Angie and her crew hang around.'

I tried to laugh it off but Joyce caught my nervous reaction. 'Did he ask you to explain why you were there?'

She knew this was uncharted territory for us. I had told Joyce a little about Angie and my marrying Isabella, but not everything. She had left it to me to tell my girlfriend Belisa about it in my own time, in my own way. But she still didn't know about me driving all the cash around with

Mateo, and my casual criminality. It was time Joyce knew everything too.

After I'd laid my whole life out on the line for the second time in one day I felt a sudden feeling of exhaustion. Joyce, to her credit, didn't trip or even betray her feelings. She nodded along as I told her how I thought I was doing a good deed by helping Angie's kid out in case her mom got pinched, and how I didn't take their money. I went on to discuss how I knew now, after realizing these two separate worlds of the mafia and music were about to brutally intersect, that I had to bring the actual criminal part of my life to an end.

It felt arduous but enlightening to relive what I had done in the last few months. In the retelling I realized that I was making gradual progress. Progressing to my goal of being a professional musician was at stake, and Joyce didn't pull any punches. 'If there was a sign meant for you to see, this might be it, Huey,' she smiled.

I had known that the way things were going with the band would mean I'd have to stop dabbling in the street shit. But Fred clocking me downtown was a harbinger of my carelessness. Why hadn't I thought about these two parts of my life ever intersecting? Making a change was inevitable, but it was also very difficult for me to imagine how I was going to finesse this situation. 'Sign of the times, Joyce,' I quipped. I had reached a decision about how to proceed. I was feeling hopeful and I told Joyce as much: 'I'm not an official member or anything like that, and, technically, I don't take a cut, so . . .' I looked to Joyce for confirmation that all was going to be ok.

But instead she came back with, 'So, it won't be like a divorce?'

I hadn't forgotten that I had to stay married for a few more years to make it look like a real-deal marriage. I wanted to honour that commitment, and I would, but I could do without the extra errands I ran for Angie. I just had to figure out how to tell Angie I was going to move on. 'It might be,' I frowned at the thought of disappointing Angie. 'I just don't know yet.'

I could feel myself starting to stress out from thinking about all the variables at play in my very complicated life, and I told Joyce as much.

She came back with a doozie. 'I can help you sort through the feelings you have. Eventually you'll get a clearer picture of what is in store for you when you do make that cut.' Her eyes met mine while she said, 'But it will be your shot to take.'

I laughed. 'That is some gangster shit, Joyce.'

'Well, kid, I'm not your lawyer.' It was her turn to laugh. 'I'm your gangster shrink.'

Chapter Seventeen

Astoria

A round the time the Angie RICO stuff was going down (in the end she dodged it with the help of a good lawyer) I moved out of the apartment I was sharing with Fast and his boy 'Gabe', a graphic designer, in downtown Brooklyn. The loft we rented on Park Avenue South had become untenable. Fast was a cool guy, but we were very different people, of different ages, and it was a good thing for us and the band to not be living under the same roof anymore.

My girlfriend Belisa had a childhood friend named Chris who was looking to find a new place with a roommate and, after some nudging from her, I gave him a call. Chris was a bass player and we hit it off immediately. We both loved punk music and talked for hours on the refined aspects of Cro-Mags' *The Age of Quarrel* album. We found a nice two-bedroom place in Astoria, Queens, and moved in. After a few months Chris decided to get a place closer to Manhattan and moved on, leaving me and Sugar the whole crib.

Astoria is an old-school Greek immigrant neighbourhood north-east of Manhattan, right near Astoria Park on the East River. The place we rented was on a quiet leafy street half a block from the park. The hood was really mellow and only a few blocks from the subway I took into the city when I didn't get a ride from Mateo. Our crib was the second floor of a red-brick house that had been renovated into two separate apartments over two floors.

Our landlord was a big Greek bruiser we called 'Mr T'. His name was something longer and unpronounceable, but most folks didn't bother to go all the way. The neighbours downstairs were a lesbian couple, Katie and Lourdes, who later told me they'd both contracted HIV from needles. They had two daughters who were about seven years old when I moved in. The two 'moms' had become a couple after they had both experienced some really tough times with male partners, and their little family was the result of a lot of hard struggle and perseverance. Katie and Lourdes were very cool, and we used to smoke joints together all the time. That's when they told me about the HIV. It didn't bother me at all and we became really good friends after passing through that portal.

I know some people are wary of people with HIV but Lourdes and Katie were very open about it. We talked about the stigma involved and how their kids (the girls were bio-logically Lourdes') would have to learn to live with their parents possibly dying early and all the other shit that went along with it.

The day I signed my record deal I had quietly celebrated with Katie and Lourdes in their apartment, drinking Rémy Martin and smoking weed in my small kitchen while the kids slept downstairs. The rest of my band were doing something else and didn't really socialise with me much anymore. Katie and Lourdes were genuinely happy for me and we talked about recording the album and my having their kids come through the studio. They were really good mothers; the way they wanted their girls to experience different things when they were young was reminiscent of how my mother raised me. I really loved those crazy chicks.

One day, not long after the deal had been signed and the cheques had been cut and cashed, I came home after buying a leather jacket on Broadway to find Lourdes and Katie waiting for me.

Katie told me Mr T had come by and was very upset. He told Katie he thought I was 'up to no good' and that he wasn't going to let a drug dealer mess up his neighbourhood.

'*What?!*' I sat down on our stoop out front.

'Yeah, he was bugging,' Katie sat down beside me, lighting a joint. 'He was tripping about all the boxes you put out for the recycling.' She pointed over to the many empty Marshall boxes folded by the side of the house.

I had arranged for all the equipment I had bought for the album recording to be delivered to my house, not thinking it might set off any alarms with my hyper-vigilant landlord. But I now realized that two huge Marshall stacks, three or four guitars, a bunch of electronics and cables and their boxes could have looked like something nefarious to someone suspicious.

'So he thinks I'm . . .' I let it trail off. I had to talk to Mr T before he called the cops or did something crazy.

Later that evening Mr T beat me to it. I was eating a well-done sausage-and-pepperoni pizza from the good pizza place on Ditmars Boulevard in my kitchen when I heard some commotion out front. Shit. I watched as Mr T and two of his sons, who I knew, loudly got out of a Lincoln Town Car at the curb. What immediately put me on guard was what Mr T's son, Agamemnon, was holding like a bunch of flowers by his side.

A shotgun.

I made for the door. I wanted to meet them before they were ready, not because I wanted to get shot, but because they wouldn't be resolved to let off the gun before they knew the score. Given what they thought I was up to, I could have had ten thugs chilling inside with me, all armed with AK-47s for all they knew. I also thought I had a good relationship with Mr T and felt pretty confident that if I had a few moments to talk to him, I could assuage his concerns.

I peeked through the peephole on the front door. The boys were walking behind their father, which I took as a good sign. Mr T wasn't a dummy and would want to know what was happening in his property before he made any rash decisions. I watched them through the peephole again and timed it so I opened the door just as Mr T's right hand was reaching for the doorbell.

Ding-dong!

As the door opened, Mr T didn't flinch. He widened his eyes a little in surprise, but that was it. This guy was a cool customer who wasn't easily rattled. Mr T acknowledged my outstretched hand, shook it and nodded hello.

'Huey, you going somewhere?' he whispered to me, barely audible. We were in the foyer of the house and the stairs to my unit were right next to where Lourdes and Katie's front door was. He was being quiet so as not to be noticed by them, though I was pretty sure they would have their ears up to the door with a glass or something, listening in. That thought made me more uncomfortable. I worried that if something went wrong and Agamemnon let off the 12-gauge they might be hurt. So I acted quickly to defuse the situation.

'Hello, Mr T. To the contrary,' I said in my clearest English, 'I was expecting you. Please do come up.' I looked over to Agamemnon and his apparently unarmed brother,

Lysander, to see if they were inclined to join their father. Before I turned, I heard Mr T say something in Greek ending in '*malaka*', which I assumed was aimed at me. The boys relaxed a little but gave me a look to say if I did anything to their daddy, I was dead. Agamemnon lowered his shotgun to his side and Lysander lit a black cigarette.

'Why do you have all of this expensive electronic things being brought here?' Mr T asked me in broken English.

'Let me show you.' I walked up the flight of stairs to my apartment. When we got to the doorway, I raised my arm to allow Mr T to go in first.

'Fuck that,' Mr T growled, shoving me roughly into my apartment. He then shouted something else in Greek down to his sons, which made both boys run up to us on the landing. I regained my balance and tried to do the same to my composure. I did not like this old fuck manhandling me. And his two sons were a hair away from . . .

'Gentlemen,' I barely managed. 'Let me show you the reason why I have all this stuff being delivered.' I walked into the kitchen and over to the counter. By the phone was my EMI record contract, which I picked up and handed to Mr T.

'This is my recording contract with EMI Records, North America,' I was laying it out, as if to a child. I did not want any confusion considering a shotgun was present. Mr T looked at the contract like it was a trick.

'What is this paper?' he scoffed. 'This is why you deal drugs and get big money to buy expensive shit?' He was getting worked up thinking I was playing him. Getting nowhere, I thought it best to appeal to the peanut gallery: his sons.

'Aggie, you know what a record deal is, right?' I asked Agamemnon. Agamemnon was a little pudgy with longish hair like he was in the band Oasis, and always seemed to have a greasy sheen to his face. He looked at his father, who nodded his assent.

'Yeah? Why?' he answered.

'Because, Aggie, I have one right here.' I pointed to the contract in his father's hand.

Mr. T held it out for me to take like it was a grenade, so I did.

'Thank you, sir.' I nodded at Mr T, whose confusion could turn to anger very quickly, so I kept on cooking.

'You can see it says "recording agreement" right there on the top.' I pointed at the contract but kept eye contact on these guys just in case it all kicked off. 'And here is my name, "Hugh Thomas Morgan".' I was looking over at Mr T, now appealing to his reason. 'This is my dream come true, Mr T.' I held his gaze. 'Sir, I have been working for this my whole life . . .'

I guess I was compelling enough for him because after a few more examples of this Mr T made a sound like a steam engine coming to an abrupt stop. 'Jesus H. Christ, Huey! I think you are bringing drugs and shit here . . .' He was waving his hands at Agamemnon now, embarrassed he had him bring a gun. 'Please, Aggie, lower that fucking thing, *malaka* . . .'

Turning back to me with his hands in prayer, he said, 'I think such bad things about you, but you are not motherfuck dealer.' Now he was ushering the boys out of the apartment, apologizing as he did so. He was making to leave and I followed him out. 'Please, Huey, you know I'm not a madman crazy person. These things made me think bad of you.' He was pointing to the boxes by the side of the house. 'I am very sorry for this,' he said, from the stoop again, with the praying hands. By now, his two sons were waiting for him by the car; the shotgun had magically vanished from sight.

'Sure, man, I get it,' I managed, but the adrenaline dump I was experiencing was playing with my head so much that I had to sit down on the stoop and light a cigarette.

'You ok?' Mr T asked, now concerned for my welfare. I was just processing the chemicals running through my body and didn't really give a fuck enough to answer him. Mr T took that as my reasonable exasperation at his recent behaviour and shrugged it off: 'Ok, my boy, let's be friends again like we were before, yes?'

If it hadn't been for my recent sojourn into therapy, I would have soundly declined. But my new outlook on life had given me a much-needed perspective I didn't have before. 'Sure,' I said through gritted teeth. 'We're good.'

And at that Mr T smiled like everything was ok, patted me on my shoulder as I sat listless on my stoop. He ambled over to his black Lincoln and then, just like Dr Zhivago, he turned and smiled. I wanted to flip him off but I was tired so I smiled back. It took less effort.

As his car's red lights turned off the block, Katie came out on the stoop and sat down. She was smiling at her Chuck Taylors.

'What?' I asked.

'You should be an actor . . .' She laughed now, smoke billowing.

'Like De Niro?' I made that face Bob De Niro makes, squinting and looking around. We both laughed for a while and then I remembered my pizza. 'Yo, girl, I got a half a pie from the good place up on Ditmars – you want a slice?'

Katie paused to think, then pulled a face. 'You talkin' to me?'

Chapter Eighteen

My New Family

Growing up I didn't really have a family like other people do, it was just my mother and I. But when I was in the Marines I suddenly had a huge family of almost 200,000 crazy brothers. I found a sense of security in that: for the first time in my life, I felt part of something that valued me. Now that I was trying to build my own musical family of brothers with Fun Lovin' Criminals, I wanted to make something that could weather any storm the music business could throw at us. Whenever you hear stories about how bands break up it is almost always about the money – either that, or some Australian stripper. I wanted to avoid that and do things the right way from the off.

The conversation came after Steve, Fast and I had just finished a meeting at EMI with Mike Schnapp and Larry Braverman. Larry was our product manager and another mensch. We had discussed how I would be responsible for our image, something that was very important to me. How the band looked and sounded was very much my vision. My guys Fast and Steve were fine with it – and now so was EMI.

We finished the meeting with the understanding that Davitt was keeping a 'hands-off' approach to us regarding image and sound. We were already producing the album ourselves, and now that autonomy spilled over to the other stuff. The band's sound and look and overall image was already conceived in my head, and I made clear to the label what my vision for Fun Lovin' Criminals was: the band always in suits, paying homage not only to the bluesmen I admired growing up but also a little gangster flair. No last names were to be used and the image wasn't too serious either – a fine line to walk. Over the previous few months, my detailed discussions with Mike and Davitt had given them the impression I knew what I was doing. I didn't really, but I knew on a gut level how to be authentic and was confident in my own taste. Once I got through my head that EMI were not humouring me by giving me a record deal, it was smooth sailing.

With Mike's help I hired two very accomplished graffiti artists who had crossed over to graphic design to help me realize my vision. Dr Revolt famously spray-painted the *Wild Style* movie poster and even appeared in the film, and Gerb had just made it big with his art co-operative GFS. That was 'Gerb', 'Futura 2000' and 'Stash'. These cats did the whole Philly Blunt revival and they were riding a wave. A meeting was arranged to get everyone together to talk about the album art. We had a great art team set up to keep it all authentically New York City, and I was directing them to find all the obscure but really cool aspects of art in NYC. It was a part of the job I hadn't anticipated and I found it one of the most enjoyable. As a kid I loved art and my mom took me to all types of art exhibitions. From the MoMA to some SoHo gallery with Basquiats and Haring's on the wall, I loved art and this part was very fun. We had world famous graffiti writer Dr Revolt with us and he blessed us with some amazing stuff.

Now to family business.

After the record company meeting, I took the band to smoke a joint behind the CBS Records 'Black Rock' building, just next door to EMI. The meeting had gone really well and this cat Henry, who was the EMI art director, loved all of my ideas and approaches to the album and its imagery. We had all felt a great sense of excitement and that came with us outside. There was a cool little alleyway cut out between the two blocks from where you could see into Mr Chow's restaurant on the ground floor, which always made the clientele visibly irritated. Mike had taken me to the alley a few times before to blaze a joint, and the place was usually quiet enough to have a business meeting and a smoke on a

Wednesday afternoon. I kicked things off, telling the guys about the design idea I had for the CD, which was to use an image of a roulette wheel. With joint poised I said, 'I think we can even get the roulette wheel printed on the vinyl, in the middle where the writing is.'

Steve accepted the doobie, took a puff . . . and held it. His Goth attire had been recently retired and he now wore a New York Jets jersey and beanie, looking like a homie. He coughed out, 'I have a machine where I can't see the CD when it plays. So do a lot of people I know.'

Fast tutted and laughed. His dark Midas Mufflers corduroy baseball cap was covering his longish hair. With his baggy jeans and hoodie, he looked like a gangly gas station attendant from Tennessee. 'When you pop the cover on the player to change the disc the CD is still spinnin', right?' he asked.

Steve made a silly face and pretended to be amazed by Fast's revelation. 'Oh fuck, yeah, it does . . .' Steve was from upstate New York, where they have a distinct way of emphasizing words most other humans would not. Steve's affectation was his way off letting us know he got the idea about the CD spinning around to simulate a roulette wheel.

We paused to let a security guard do his walk through the alley without making a nuisance of ourselves. We liked this spot and wanted to be able to keep using it as our office. Once the security guy turned the corner, I relit the jay. It was time for the main talk. As I spoke, I changed my tone.

I felt like I was back briefing my Marines. 'I was talking to Fred Davis about the publishing,' I explained, 'and he wants us to give him the breakdowns for the publishing contract he's negotiating. Y'all know. Like, who wrote what, shit like that,' I had my plan about how I wanted to proceed but I wanted to see what the boys had in mind first. A good leader, I remembered from the Marines, takes the temperature before he talks.

Steve spoke first. 'The way I understand it is you break it down to who wrote what, right?' He was looking across at me and Fast as he spoke. Steve had sobered up a little, as had Fast.

'Yeah, take "King of New York".' It was Fast's turn to speak. 'You wrote the basic music stuff, with the Deodato sample, loop, horns. And me and Huey did some shit too.' Fast glanced over at me to confirm what he was saying. I nodded. 'So that's like 70 per cent to you, right?' Fast was getting into his flow now. 'Me and Huey then split the other 30 per cent.'

Steve was holding another hit of weed smoke in, so I took the opportunity to speak. 'That's cool for the music part, Fast, but from what Fred told me the song is split when it comes to words and music. That's what I wanted to talk about in detail with you guys.' The fact that I was five years older than them meant Fast and Steve looked up to me and trusted me when it came to things like this. I understood that and I wanted to let them know I wasn't abusing that trust to pull a fast one, no pun intended. 'The way I see it, we are all in this together.' I took the joint from Fast and gave them what I hoped was a sincere look. 'Yeah, I could play it like the lawyer wants, take 70 per cent of all the publishing and that wouldn't even be what I deserved if you broke it down song by song. If I write all the lyrics, that's half of every song. Then there's tracks like "Methadonia" and "Coney Island Girl", which I wrote by myself, so that's even more for me on this album . . .'

As I spoke I was looking at Steve and Fast in the eyes, watching for their tells. I may have known these guys in a pedestrian sense, but you don't know anyone fully, especially not when it comes to money. I was laying it all out for them and taking extra time to see if they were understanding what I was offering them.

It was time to make my play.

'How's this?' I paused for effect. 'I was taught in the Marines to lead from the front, so here it is . . .' Another pause, more eye contact. This was very important for them to understand. 'I think the only way for us to go on as brothers and as a band is that we all get an equal cut of everything from here on out.'

Fast's eyes gave him away: he didn't think I had it in me to be so generous. That made me laugh a little inside, but I kept going. 'Thirty-three and a motherfuckin' third!' I shouted.

Steve passed me the joint as a form of answer. 'My man, you sure? I mean, that's a big fuckin' gesture . . .' he stammered, in shock.

He didn't say that I didn't need to make that 'big fuckin' gesture', but that was it, wasn't it? I was the man, and the man doesn't need it all.

The man needs loyalty though.

I was giving these guys, my new family, an equal cut in this venture. It was worth it to me to know that they felt valued and appreciated beyond their most reasonable expectations. An equal share was my price for that solace.

Having got over their shock, now the boys properly responded.

'Huey, man, we're gonna rock this shit!' Steve came forwards first, hugging me like a brother. He was getting emotional. I understand a few things very well, and sincerity is one of them.

I hugged him back in a bear hug-type grapple. 'We are, Steve-o! All the way, bro!'

Even Fast, who is socially challenged, got in on the moment. 'We're like a real bunch of gay boys, hugging and shit.' He was laughing as we gave pounds and handshakes all around, but he was also looking uncomfortably around in case someone was eavesdropping.

I watched him and his self-consciousness do a few loops and thought about all the variables at play. I wondered how these variables had come together to make this band happen. How did my vision of a hybrid hip-hop/rock project that could both discuss meaningful issues and bring the dope grooves somehow meet these weird social reject techno enthusiasts? And how in the hell did that musical monstrosity get into the ears of a record company so much that a major label had given us *carte blanche*?

I also thought that I was right about their motivations. The only way these cats were going to tolerate me steering the whole thing was equity. 'Partners in crime' is too easy a moniker, but it fitted. We all did things musically in this band that the others didn't and couldn't, and we all had clear roles. That was the magic of being in the FLC.

But the roles outside of the music had to be defined as well. Which is why we needed to embark on this adventure into the unknown on an equal footing where the rubber met the road: the money. From now on, whenever I made a decision about something non-musical concerning the FLC, I wouldn't worry my motives would be questioned by the boys, because we would all benefit equally no matter what deal I cut. The split made sense to me on a whole bunch of levels, and I was really happy the boys were seeing things my way.

I had a captive audience now so I continued to break it down for them, holding my fingers out one at a time as I went. 'Publishing is one thing we split three ways.'

One finger.

'Royalties from future sales are split too.'

Another finger.

'Boom!' from Steve. He was happy.

'We also split the tour profits and merchandise.' I stopped counting to light a cigarette. 'Which reminds me. I have an idea for a windbreaker that has FLC on it like the FBI ones. Blue with the yellow letters – it's gonna sell like hotcakes.'

Steve laughed at that. 'Yeah,' he nodded. 'I think it's amazing you're getting merch ideas together now.'

Fast, meanwhile, was staring into the middle distance, thinking. I could tell he was looking for holes in my proposal. You could almost hear the gears in his head going around. But I was cool with that. I would have done the same exercise if I were him, just not so awkwardly.

I guess how Fast grew up had a lot to do with how he became so weird. He's a cool guy, a bit nerdy, from the suburbs above New York City where life is soft. He wasn't used to people appreciating and trusting him, and that made him very suspicious. Even though I had told him in the past that I would look out for him – and had – he was still looking for what he might be missing in my offer. This was a huge deal for him, and he didn't want to fuck it up.

'Why, bro?' He finally came back from his reverie into wherever. 'If Fred says we should be accurate about the split, why are you making it even?'

Fast was genuinely unable to make it make sense in

his mind. Initially I figured he was surprised at my altruism. But, as he went on, I knew it was more than that. 'If I wrote a whole song, that's all mine, bro. I wouldn't . . .' He stopped talking because his brain had finally caught up with his mouth.

I knew right then that Fast didn't have the same idea about what being on this adventure was all about. It didn't matter that much to my plan, because once he did get what the fuck I was talking about he would realize I still was looking out for him like I was his big brother – even if he felt differently about that now. His paranoiac ways would be something he and I would revisit on many occasions in the future. For now, I tried to get the ball back by accentuating the positive: 'When all the shit is done, we can make this album and go play gigs and do what we want to do!' That was why I was here: to do what I wanted when I wanted. That was 'rock and roll'. That freedom was the whole fucking point.

'We are the three luckiest guys we know,' I summarized, with an edge to my voice, pointing my finger at them both in turn. 'We've got to stick together, which is why I think the even split is the only way to go, my bros.' I smiled the last couple of words to try to take the Marine out of it. But not completely: I had to let them know this was kindness from strength, not some other set of circumstances.

Proper motivation makes you stronger in your mind and

that translates to everything else. Despite the ganja they had smoked, Fast and Steve both nodded soberly at my pep talk. They looked like guys who knew they were genuinely valued. Job done.

Chapter Nineteen

$6000 Delay

The studio we chose to record our debut album was called the Magic Shop. The studio was contained in a time capsule of a building that emanated old-school New York cool. Located on a quiet cobblestoned street, it was in the middle of SoHo between Spring and Broome streets and was the perfect recording studio for me in every way.

The Magic Shop was a throwback to an era when musicians spent a great deal of time in the studio looking for the perfect guitar sound or the most comfortable chair. It boasted a unique and quite beautiful BBC Neve broadcast/recording console from the sixties – all the other recording gear was vintage too. Vox and Fender amps that looked like the stuff the Beatles used were all for the taking. Burnt sienna linen wallpaper and dark wood on the console and studio accents kept the vibe very organic, which was one of the reasons I wanted to record the album there. We were trying to mix a very new type of sample-heavy project that needed to sonically differentiate itself from its digital origins. The constant reminders to 'keep it analogue' were really helpful in finding that balance.

Three weeks into recording the album, Davitt Siegerson and Mike Schnapp asked to hear some of the tunes we'd tracked. I was worried these weren't final mixes at all, but Mike assured us Davitt fully understood the album-making process and wouldn't be making any conclusions when he came through to 'just hang'.

We had been wasting no time in recording all the music. In fact, we finished most of the initial tracking in just five days. Day one had been a 'getting to know you' day with Tim Latham, our engineer extraordinaire. He got the tape machines calibrated with Sean, our assistant engineer, and then we dropped all the samples and sequences onto the two-inch tape just in time for dinner. Little Charlie's Clam Bar was a Little Italy institution and we ordered dinner from there at least three times a week. The fried shrimp and linguini was world class, though you had to order the medium sauce; the hot sauce was inedible, and I say that as someone who loves his spicy food.

I was having the time of my life learning about all the gear and techniques. I was like a sponge when it came to the process of recording, just like when I was a kid with my TASCAM Portastudio. Tim was extremely generous with his knowledge and time, teaching me a Ph.D amount of stuff as we recorded all the basic tracks. Day two involved building a drum 'tent' with baffle blankets and some super-funky-looking sound screens on wheels from the 1960s. After guitar day (three), keyboard day (four) and vocal day (five), we realized all we had left to record were some random percussion tracks for a handful of songs, and my lead vocals.

This realisation allowed us to relax and not stress about having the head of the label and our A&R guy come through to hang out. We even did a few rough mixes for tunes we were almost ready to cross off the big board for them to listen to. In the control room we had a big white board where we'd keep tabs of what we had recorded so far. Instead of doing one song at a time, we got ourselves a great drum sound that would work for the whole album, and we took it from there. This process saved a lot of time; I'd decided to go down this route because deep down I worried that EMI might just pull the plug on the whole fucking operation when they heard what we were up to. Not that we were making bad music, or anything like that; it was more that neither myself, Tim nor the band had ever heard anything like this music before at this level. If what the Sex Pistols once said about EMI was even partly true, we had to cover our asses.

*

The spring evening that Davitt and Mike came down was warm enough to have the door to the studio open. We were hanging out front like it was the Ravenite Social Club when they arrived. I was wearing a wife-beater and smoking a cigarette in a folding chair when Mike's big Caddy ended its peregrination across the cobblestones. Next to Mike, along the huge white sofa, adjusting his white Polo baseball cap, was the CEO of EMI, Davitt Sigerson. Mike's Caddy was the coolest fucking car ever, and if these two dudes alighting from it could only have been caught on film, it would have won an Oscar. Although the pair were polar opposites, in a cop/buddy film kind of way, they looked bad ass as hell. Mike was rocking jeans and a Slayer t-shirt while Davitt – in his open-at-the-neck British tailored, cutaway-collared white shirt and stiff blue jeans with ironed crease – brought the classiness downtown.

'Gentlemen, welcome to Magic Shop . . .' I crooned.

I was living my best life and it was a particularly beautiful spring evening in SoHo, one that felt full of possibility. Mike and Davitt were in good spirits too. There was something to the moody musician cliché and they – and we – were all happy to be the exception to that rule.

'Huey, my man,' Mike beamed. 'How are ya?' His big baritone finished with a roar.

'I'm great.' I gave Mike an overly complicated handshake and turned to Davitt. 'Big man . . . Big D!'

I have always taken great joy in giving people nicknames. I do it all the time because it's a way to endear people to me. How they make me feel is the criterion as to how cool the nickname I bestow on them is.

Davitt was painfully awkward with us 'homies', so I took it easy as far as the handshake went. He pulled out a thin Cuban cigar, which I lit with my USMC Zippo lighter. 'Sorry about all the lighter fluid, D,' I apologized for the Zippo and its pungent aroma. 'It's kind of breezy tonight, and if you wanna blaze up, this is the only realistic option . . .'

Davitt waved my concern off with his free hand and puffed the stogie to life. Then he straightened. 'This is a scene, isn't it?' he said as he looked around.

It was indeed a picturesque block: quiet, warm and welcoming, the cobblestones lit by soft yellow streetlights gave it a frozen-in-time feel. We took a moment to take it in, each of us in turn giving the vista an approving nod. 'Good shit,' I managed to surmise. I flicked my cigarette into the street and raised my arm like a movie usher. 'Shall we . . .?' Davitt and then Mike passed through the doorway into the Magic Shop.

Here goes nothing, I thought.

'You guys have met Tim,' I gave our engineer a pound as I leaned over the console to where he was positioned. Fast and Steve had gone inside and were lounging on the sofa at the back of the room and they got up to greet Mike and Davitt. When all the hellos were over, I showed Mike and Davitt to some chairs by a high 'producer's desk' behind Tim.

The recording desk was constructed as a semi-circle, where the engineer sits in its centre surrounded by the obligatory faders and knobs. When we all got settled I asked Tim to play a few songs for our guests: we'd worked up rough mixes of 'I Can't Get With That', 'The Grave and the Constant' and 'King of New York' for them to listen to.

As the opening bars of 'I Can't Get With That' filled the studio I was amazed at how good everything sounded on the 'big boys', the huge studio speakers that were fitted into the walls either side of the recording console. Because I had my eyes closed listening for everything all at once I missed Davitt rising from his seat at the end of the song. The guitar solo at the end was a recent addition and I thought I had done a really good job on it. Turned out Davitt thought so too.

'Jesus H. Christ, Huey!' I opened my eyed to see Davitt pumping his hand in the air like he was at a concert. 'You brought that one home!'

Davitt was someone who was pretty reserved most of the time, so his enthusiasm at hearing our music was encouraging, to say the least. I was still smiling like a mook at the accolade as 'King of New York' started up.

Mike and Davitt shut up as the drum-roll intro dropped us

all into that low-down funk groove. Now it was Davitt's turn to close his eyes. I watched him vibing along, bobbing his head in time. Mike looked over to me and the boys leaning at the back wall smoking cigarettes. 'This is my favourite,' he said as the trumpets brought us to the chorus.

'La-di da-di, free John Gotti, indeed . . .' Davitt added as the song faded out. 'That sound, the Rhodes?' Davitt looked over at Fast, who nodded.

'Yeah, it's a Rhodes,' he affirmed, the cigarette smoke creating a halo around his head.

'It sounds like *Trouble Man*, the way it keeps the time . . .' Davitt was not just a hands-on label boss but also a hugely successful record producer. He had a lot of stuff to talk to us about, and I was flattered he cared as much as he apparently did.

'That's my favourite Marvin album, D,' I joined in the conversation. The boys were shy around adults and Tim, who hated all record label employees, was keeping quiet so as not to say something offensive to our esteemed visitors.

'That is such a great hook!' Davitt was still very excited about the music. Then he asked about the trumpets that play a big part in the aesthetic of the song. 'Are those . . . real trumpets?' He was holding his right hand to his mouth emulating playing the trumpet.

'Yes, they are . . .' I turned to Fast, who looked like he got caught doing something wrong.

'This guy played 'em.' I gave Fast his flowers. 'When we got into the studio to start recording this song we didn't know this guy even played the horn.'

I was pointing to Fast now, who was visibly uncomfortable with me doing so, but I didn't care. I continued my anecdote. 'We were talking one day after lunch, and Tim was telling us about how he went to Berklee for bass.' Berklee School of Music is a well-known music college in Boston. 'When I asked Fast what he went to college for he just said he went to Syracuse University for "music" . . .' I was setting it up nicely. Fast was squirming a little at being the subject of conversation but kept quiet. 'This fucking guy . . .' I laughed at Fast, who finally cracked a smile. 'I ask him, "What kind of 'music'? Piano, keys, that shit, right?"'

Fast started to giggle at this point, so I finished up.

'He goes, "Nah, Huey, I went to school for trumpet."'

'That's Fast?' Mike Schnapp chimed in, surprised as hell at my revelation.

'Yeah, Mike, fucking trumpet player over here forgot to tell us of his virtuosity.' I deadpan the rest. 'So I ask him where this trumpet is.'

I turned to Fast, who threw his hands up in the air. 'I didn't think it was that important, until this . . .' Fast pointed at the speakers.

'So I ask him where this trumpet is, and he says it's at his mom and dad's house down in North Carolina.' Fast's parents had recently moved from the leafy suburbs of New York City to the even leafier suburbs of Raleigh.

Fast was smiling but still squirming because he was in the spotlight, a place he wasn't yet comfortable being in. 'Yeah,' he nodded, 'I called up my dad and asked him to FedEx that shit up here, and bam!'

It was indeed a revelation for us as a band to have a guy who as well as playing keys, bass and sequences, now also played trumpet as well. I gave Fast a complicated handshake and we calmed down enough for Davitt to circle back.

'Can we hear that one again?' he asked.

I nodded to Tim when he looked to me for the ok.

'Sure, D. Hit it, Tim,' I said and lit a smoke.

When the song finished a second time, Davitt turned to Tim. 'Could you please rewind that again to the top of the second chorus?'

Tim looked at me again for approval. The idea that a label guy could order around the recording engineer didn't sit well with him. Davitt clocked it too and laughingly admitted, 'I'm sorry, yes, studio protocol.' He gave Tim a salute and turned to me. 'I'd love to hear the second chorus, *Huey*.'

I looked back at Tim, who was waiting for me to say something. I nodded and he began finding the spot in the song Davitt wanted to hear again. The sound of music slowing down and speeding up at a low volume filled the room as the machine that synched the two 24-track tape machines together did its stuff. The synch machine kept whining a little longer than usual so I threw a disposable lighter that was on the desk by my ashtray at it. It struck the machine with a crack and immediately the two tape machines synched up. The chorus came through the huge speakers again.

As we listened I watched Davitt, his eyes closed, listening intently to my song.

When the chorus was over he opened his eyes and found me in the room. 'Can I get that once more please?' he asked, all polite. Davitt knew that the studio was where you laid out your heart and soul, and to be blasé about its sensitivities was surely not the way of the Samurai.

'Sure, D.' Another nod to Tim and a comedic eye-roll to my guys Fast and Steve, who were smoking on the sofa behind me and starting to look a little nervous.

The chorus came and went and Davitt asked for it to be played again. After the fourth listen he turned to me and the boys. 'You know that delay on the lead vocal in the chorus?' He was engaging us like a bro and I appreciated him for that. The boys, who didn't know what to make of this guy and all his questions, looked over at me to answer.

'Yeeaah?' I replied slowly. What was he getting at? Tim caught my eye and his look told me that he didn't like this shit either.

'How attached are you to it?' Davitt asked, point blank.

'Why?' I asked, again not seeing his point.

'I'd love to hear the chorus without the delay on the lead vocal . . . if that's not too much trouble?' The last request was aimed at Tim, who gave Davitt a wry look and sighed.

'Tim, can you pop that delay off the LV for Davitt, please?' I asked. I'm always polite in the studio because when you spend a lot of time with people in a creative environment, it pays to be gracious.

Tim rolled the song's chorus without the delay and we all listened intently.

'Huey, how attached are you to that delay on the vocal in the chorus?' Davitt was being serious and so I answered seriously back.

'I thought it helped move the lyric in that part, you know, like an old-school hip-hop delay.'

Davitt nodded and processed the information for a minute. He then asked me something I hadn't anticipated. 'If I asked you to consider removing it, how would you respond?' Davitt leaned back in his chair to let his question wash over me and my ego. I could tell he was challenging me to look at this from his perspective. I wasn't sure I was able to do that. I took a moment to think while Fast, Steve, Tim and Mike looked around the control room uncomfortably. Would this delay make a huge difference to how the song sounded? Would acquiescing to his whim set a precedent that I, as a producer, would have to negotiate every time Davitt didn't agree with me on a production element? Head of the label or not, I decided to roll up on Davitt like I would on anyone who wanted something for nothing. 'I'm sure that the song will survive the delay being removed. But what is it worth to you . . .' I paused to let my comment land the right way '. . . to have it taken off?'

I was looking directly at Davitt as I spoke, not in a physically challenging way, but to ensure he understood I was not in a position of weakness. I had just signed a huge contract that ensured that me and my band had full creative control over the final mix of our album. I knew Davitt was well aware of this too.

Davitt smiled back at me, his look belying his view of me as his apprentice, now rising to the challenge. He took a moment to make sure I understood his motivations.

'One thousand dollars?' he asked.

I scrunched up my face and replied almost instinctively, 'Two thousand . . .'

Davitt looked like he was at a three-card monte game, his eyes confused at the speed of my hustle. For a moment all the air in the room was still, no one daring to speak for fear of breaking the spell I had cast.

Finally, after what seemed like an eternity, Davitt succumbed. 'Ok, I guess . . . Two thousand dollars it is, then,' he said, clearly relieved the haggle was over.

You could tell this guy wasn't a street dude by the way he caved in so quick. So I took this initiative. 'Each,' I added.

'Each?' Davitt shot back, not relieved anymore.

'Yeah, I can't take your two Gs and look my boys in the eye, can I?' I was goading Davitt now that I had won the big balls contest he started. Davitt looked from me to Fast and then to Steve, smiling. He looked a little uncomfortable, but you could tell he was having a good time here in the trenches with the troops.

'Him too?' Davitt pointed at Tim, who we all knew couldn't stand, 'record company types', as he called them.

I laughed at that and let him off the hook.

'Nah, we pay Tim. But, yeah, two Gs all around.' I was making the hand gesture for another round of drinks.

Davitt was still looking like a guy who was having a good time despite losing six grand over a delay on a vocal. He turned to Mike Schnapp. 'Tell legal to cut each of these gentlemen a cheque tomorrow morning for two thousand dollars.'

By this point, Fast and Steve were looking at me like I was Moses, or someone like that. Davitt turned back to me and said, 'I think that the song is better served by losing that delay, and if it takes me putting my money where my mouth is, so be it.' He stuck out his hand and we shook on it.

'Yo, Tim.' Tim looked up at me from his desk and nodded. 'Lose it,' I told him.

Tim removed the delay patch from the vocal track and we then wrapped up the visit. I walked Davitt and Mike out to the Caddy and had a word by the car.

'I think that from what I heard tonight you guys are doing great,' Davitt grinned. 'The record sounds amazing and, aside from that delay . . .' He gave me a wink. 'I wouldn't change a thing.'

Mike stepped in and gave me a hug. 'My man!' he beamed. 'It sounds so fucking good, bro. Huge sound!'

You could tell Mike couldn't really read Davitt yet and was visibly relieved at his curbside revelation to me.

'Thanks, guys. I'm sure we can get this recording dusted and start mixing by the end of the month.' I decided not to tell them we'd already recorded almost everything.

As the pair got into Mike's huge yacht, I was hit by a wave of emotion. For the first time that I could remember after leaving the Marines I felt I was where I was supposed to be. It was a crazy sensation. It felt good.

I smiled at my private moment and waved them off, but not before Davitt said from the window of the Caddy, 'That was the most expensive visit to the studio I've ever made.'

I smiled at that and flicked my cigarette away as the vehicle started to move forwards. 'Come back anytime, my man!' I shouted at the taillights as they bumped over the cobblestones into the night.

Chapter Twenty

The Sit-Down

Aguy I knew in the Marines once told me that courage is just 'doing it scared'. If that was the case, I must have been about as courageous as it got. I was more nervous than I had ever been, and that is saying quite a bit.

I had written a song for Fun Lovin' Criminal's titled, 'King of New York'. The song's chorus exclaims, '*La-di da-di, free John Gotti, the King of New York!*' and after playing it for Angie, she suggested she should play it for ███████, her boyfriend. ███████ worked for a family, and the boss of that family used to be John Gotti. Angie was back home and by now up to her usual antics after the RICO thing got tossed. Without getting into the artistic endeavour shit too much, I wrote the song with more than a hint of irony. I did not know that irony is a little understood phenomenon in most parts of the United States, and this was where the 'rub' was rubbing.

Word came back that the song could piss a few of the older

guys off who were still sore about the change in management downtown. John Gotti had been famously convicted and sentenced to life in federal prison after many tries by the government, and this crazy true crime mafia story was what the song was based on. Whoever was in charge of that family had to be respectfully told about my song. I had to be seen as showing the proper amount of respect and reverence to my mother-in-law's family, and not being careless and drawing unwanted attention.

The upshot was that I was being taken to a 'sit-down' with the 'management' downtown. It was a meeting that needed to happen before my album was released to the public. I knew this meeting had to happen too, but it still didn't make this any easier. I was terrified.

It all started when I got a call from Beansie, an associate of Angie's boyfriend. He told me to meet him for a slice at Ben's on Spring and Thompson to talk about my 'new song'.

Beansie was about 35 or so, but probably older: being an outlaw made you look younger in my experience. He was wiry like the boxer he was; a couple of Golden Glove wins had got him the attention of the 'outfit' and that put him in their 'academy'. The 'academy' was a loosely affiliated crew that ran some young guys from good families who were vying for membership in the family business.

Beansie was a heavy, busting heads and doing collections

at the beginning. He was a brilliant guy who applied himself and pulled heist-type jobs on the side, away from the 'academy'. When these jobs produced great results of the cash kind, he kicked a sizable tribute up to his capo without being asked. This got him fast-tracked to membership and he got his button by the time he was just 27. That's parlance for becoming a made member of a crew, or family.

Just like in the movies, these crews have a chain of command that has to be adhered to without deviation. The breakdown of this chain of command put Beansie in the equivalent rank to 'Gunnery Sergeant', had he been in the Marines. For those not familiar with military rank structure, he was about halfway to the top.

'Do you think that those old guys who might get upset will get upset, Beans?' I asked him in that first meeting, over a slice and grape drink at the counter outside of Ben's.

'That's what ██████ reckons. He thinks you and I should resolve it before they hear about it from any place else. Angie gave me the demo tape you gave her, its good, I like it. If we have a sit-down just to say how "this is you".' He pointed up and down at me. 'They will have been told already about who you are and how you've been a friend and such beforehand. And most importantly—'

I put down my grape drink and leaned forwards. 'You gotta let them know, in no uncertain terms, that this song is in no way a negative song meaning any disrespect.'

I swallowed. I was starting to feel the weight of the situation now. 'Dude, I get why the song might ruffle some feathers . . . but actually meeting up with members of this crew? Is this a wise move?' I was feeling my stress levels rising about being forced into this shit.

Beansie, by contrast, didn't give a fuck. 'It is the move I was told to make, kid,' he replied. He didn't have to say more than that to me to make me understand that my presence was not a request.

'You like the song, though, right?' I asked Beansie as he pulled the big silver Mercedes out into traffic. He'd picked me up from Angie's apartment to take me to the 'sit-down' downtown. Over the stereo 'King of New York' was blasting out.

'You know I love my old-school shit.' Beansie hit the brakes as a cab cut us off. He gave the taxi driver a look that would stick with him for the rest of the day. 'Slick Rick the ruler!' Beansie shouted at no one in particular as we sped off again.

'You get the reference, man,' I nodded. The song's chorus had a knowing nod towards 'La Di Da Di', the eighties hip-hop classic, by Doug E. Fresh and Slick Rick, then MC Ricky D. If Beansie liked the song, I figured that couldn't hurt my case.

Beansie was wearing a burgundy velour sweatsuit with

the obligatory wife-beater tank-top underneath. A thick gold chain with a long gold horn good-luck charm finished the ensemble. As we neared the Midtown Tunnel he turned to me and spoke, his voice all serious: 'It's a brilliant lyric, the song is gonna be a hit.'

I'd been smoking a cigarette with the window down to calm my nerves. With the tunnel approaching, Beansie hit the window button and it started closing. I flicked the smoke out before the window fully shut.

'I just want you to know that I think this takes balls, kid,' Beansie smiled as the tunnel flashed past. 'But don't confuse the point. Be very clear when you talk to them, they're old school, and not in a music way. They don't like fancy talk.'

As we emerged from the Midtown Tunnel the last of the evening sun bathed the Manhattan skyline. I remember thinking how beautiful it looked, and how I couldn't silence the voice in my head wondering if I'd see it again. I watched the skyline shrink in the car's mirrors as we drove on into the hinterland of Queens County, and towards my fate.

Neighbourhoods flashed by. I tried to gather my thoughts and figure out what I was going to say. I had never met any of these guys before, and their reputations alone were enough for me to think through an attempt at escaping Beansie's spaceship and making a run for it. But how would I continue to be a musician and duck the mob at the same time? It wasn't possible: the sit-down was inevitable and I knew it.

'Huey, have you put it all together?' Beansie winked at his reflection in the rear-view, reading my mind.

'Yeah, I think I've got the gist of what to say.' Part of me was regretting not taking a Valium before leaving the house. But I'd worried the guys I was meeting would notice me being a little high and that wouldn't be good for my chances. They'd see me as just another closet junkie; and they'd know that junkies can't be trusted. 'I need them to see a guy who is just telling a story about another guy who was caught up in all the bullshit surrounding the big man, JG . . .' As I explain my thoughts to Beansie, I didn't want to jinx myself by saying John Gotti's name in the presence of a made guy. On top of that, I wasn't sure I could speak freely in anyone's car, and this was certainly one of those occasions. 'It's not really about "him", anyway,' I continued. 'It's about how people will act crazy if their excuse for doing so is justified.'

Beansie slowed the car down as he chewed through my argument. 'No, kid; too complicated,' he concluded. 'You say some shit like that and you'll lose 'em.' He turned to look at me over his gold Porsche Design sunglasses. 'Just keep it simple.'

'What do you mean?' I asked.

Beansie held up his thumb on his right hand that was on the steering wheel. 'One, it's about how people love John, and still do. Two . . .' His index finger popped up. 'It is not mocking him in any way, no disrespect, yeah, nah?'

'Yeah,' I said, keeping it all straight.

'And three . . .' Somehow he managed to pop out his pinky finger without losing control of the car. 'You remind them that you keep your mouth shut.'

His foot hit the accelerator; the coaching session was over. I felt appreciative of what Beansie just did for me, and said so.

'Shit, Huey, we're proud of what you've got going,' Beansie returned.

As we pulled up to the restaurant, Beansie gave me some final advice. 'Remember, just be brief, and be respectful. And when I give you this sign . . .' He rubbed the bottom of his chin with the back of his fingers. 'That's your cue to leave.'

We both laughed: me out of nervousness, Beansie because he knew I was shitting a brick and breaking my balls was amusing.

The restaurant was in a strip mall in a part of Queens that most people didn't even know existed. We were somewhere near JFK Airport but I didn't hear any planes. Beansie turned his Mercedes into a parking space by the loading bays at the back of the joint. The cars parked back were really nice: a few late-model Caddies and a baby blue Porsche 911. I did a quick scan to make sure this wasn't a hit, which Beansie laughed at when he figured out what I was doing. 'Jesus, Huey. It would be a huge waste of time and gas to drive you all the way out here just to clip your skinny ass.'

Maybe it was dumb to think they'd do that for what I was there for, but I felt like Tommy from *Goodfellas*, and staying safe seemed more important than what Beansie thought of me.

'Yeah, yeah, yeah . . .' I muttered and got out of the car, continuing to look around.

This whole situation was getting to my nerves, and it was starting to show. As we straightened ourselves out before entering the restaurant, Beansie gave me a last-minute pep talk. 'Remember, speak only when spoken to, then be brief and clear in your manner of speech, ok, kid?'

Everything had slowed down: I felt like I was walking through gelatin and Beansie's words came out like the adults' in *Peanuts*: '*Wah, wah, wah . . .*' He guided me to a stool by the bar as he told whoever needed to know that we were here. I had worn a dark brown suit coat, a button-up black shirt and some slacks that vaguely matched the jacket. As I waited I could feel myself sweating through the shirt.

When Beansie came back a few minutes later I was finishing up a cigarette and nursing a coke. 'Hey, kid.' Beansie didn't sit down but made it clear it was time. 'Let's go . . .'

I followed him through the main restaurant, a good size dining room with about 40 people eating. Beyond that was a private room to the left of the swinging double doors that marked the entrance to the kitchen. Beansie opened the first door and walked in first, motioning for me to follow. 'Hello, gentlemen . . .' Beansie said, 'this is Huey, and Huey . . .' He made the introductions.

In front of me sat three men. Two were about 60, and were paying less attention to me and Beansie than the tiramisu in between them on the table. The younger guy, who was maybe 40, I recognized. He was a made guy who was directly affected by my little song.

'Huey?' he asked.

'Yes, sir,' I replied, slow and even. No emotion either way, like I was ordering a beer.

'Jewish?' One of the older guys, the fatter one with the turtle neck and the gold chain, spoke up.

'No, sir.' I paused, then looked back at the younger man because he was the senior man. When you're in this kind of situation where you don't know who is the senior person, always wait and see who speaks first . . . and third.

'Please, relax.' The younger pointed to a chair next to where Beansie was pulling out another one. I sat down and waited while the two older guys spoke in Italian. I could understand most of it and it was benign enough until the tiramisu was noticed again.

'Ok . . .' The younger man called the sit-down to order. Everyone shut up and looked across at him. 'So, Beansie tells us that there's a song you sing about John. He played some of the song in his car for me, but I don't know about music, do I?' He waited for the older guys to swallow their bites of dessert and continued. 'What did you do that for?' he asked, in a tone of disappointment.

I waited a beat to make sure the other guys, who were now reminding me of the two old men from *The Muppet Show*, didn't have an addendum. 'I wrote it because of how influential he was to my generation.' I paused. I was going to continue when I remembered Beansie's advice. *Speak only when spoken to, then be brief.* I waited, which was the right call. The younger man nodded and moved on.

'Why is he the King of New York, then?' He was not looking at me but at the two old guys demolishing the pudding in the middle of the table. I could smell the Kahlúa from where I was sitting.

'It was the guy in my story who called him that because he was at the time,' I explained. The second older guy, the one not wearing the turtleneck, broke the spell by saying with his mouth full of cream, 'Paulie . . . I remember that name from the song Beansie played us . . .' He was looking at the younger man, like he was reading the Sanskrit off of a relic.

'Yeah, Paulie is the main character,' I interrupted, 'who goes on the quest to free John—'

A clatter of cutlery on plates. Everyone stopped talking and eating, and turned to stare at me. I felt a rush of blood to my head and looked over at Beansie, who was shaking his head in disbelief in my clear breach of protocol. I was about to blurt out an apology when I caught myself from digging the hole any deeper.

The younger guy saw the opening and said, 'My old friend ███, and even Beansie here, tell me you're a stand-up guy.' He held up his hand, in case I had the gall to dare interrupt him. He needn't have worried: I'd learned my lesson by now. 'But I've only just met you and I want a few more answers before I allow this. Do you need a drink?'

There it was. If there was any doubt, I now knew these guys were under the impression I was here, hat in hand, asking their permission to put this song out. I guess I had better make my play, I thought. 'Sir,' I nodded my accordance and chose my words with care, 'I am here . . . very happy to meet you and answer all of your questions honestly . . . and no thank you, sir, I'm fine with the Pellegrino.'

'So help me, God!' shouted 'Turtleneck'.

At this wise crack, the wise guys all started to laugh. I smiled like a dummy and kept my mouth shut. Beansie slapped my shoulder affectionately as he laughed along with his boys.

When the moment had passed the younger concluded the sit-down. 'Kid, you're good to sing this song. I really like it and think it keeps his memory alive . . .' He looked at the ceiling like John was upstairs, or something, and I could see he was getting misty. 'That's a good thing as far as I'm concerned.' The younger man shifted his gaze back to me. 'You have a lot of good men vouching for you today. Beansie thinks you're Paul Simon, or some such shit.' He gave Beansie a look, and Turtleneck tried to say something but the younger hushed him with his finger. 'Angie and ███████ are very proud at what you've accomplished getting to this point.'

I hadn't expected Angie's name to be dropped in this particular company. I realized this must mean that she was a very valuable member of the crew.

I was still actively shutting up and I let the younger tell me, 'Don't fuck it up with thinking we won't be watching how you handle this . . .' he searched for the right words '. . . consideration.'

He looked at me seriously for a few seconds and I held his gaze back. Then he made a face like I should say something, so I did. 'Thank you, I won't disappoint you and this . . .' I searched for the right phrase because the last word I wanted to use right now was 'favour' '. . . this *personal consideration* will be something you will not regret allowing me to have.'

On the way out to the car, Beansie seemed as relieved as I was. 'I have never seen that fucking guy so emotionally honest. Shit, Huey . . .'

I was working my way through an adrenaline dump and finally my peripheral vision was returning to me. My heartbeat settled down enough for me to manage to say, 'I did what you told me to do, bro.' I lit a cigarette through shaky fingers and blew the smoke at the stars. Beansie fished for his keys, while I made a decision. 'You know what, I'm gonna take the train back to the city from here, Beans, if that's cool?' I needed to be alone right now, not stuck in a car with a mobster. Beansie looked a little confused and then a little concerned, 'Sure, Huey, I'll drop you at the A train.'

I shook my head. 'Nah, Beans. Thanks, man, but I got a joint rolled and I'm gonna walk and smoke.'

Beansie shook his head at me like I was nuts, then climbed into his silver spaceship. As he turned the engine over, the window came down and he called me back over to him. I crouched down a bit to get close so he didn't have to shout at me to be heard. 'You did good back in there, kid. No bullshit.' Beansie grabbed my cheek in his left hand like it was in a vice. He squeezed it tight in his strong fingers and then let go. I put my hand on my face and rubbed it. As he put the car into gear, he told me, smiling, 'Too bad you're not Italian, kid . . .'

I watched him drive off into the night. Then I breathed out the first deep breath I had breathed all day, lit the joint and shuffled off to find the A train.

Chapter Twenty-One

Estranged

'Hey, it's me . . .'

By 1995 I hadn't spoken to my mother in a few years. It wasn't like we were estranged, or anything weird like that. It was just one of those things. But now I had some news that I wanted to tell her, it seemed a good time to call.

My mom had gotten remarried when I was about 16 to her high school sweetheart, someone she'd been reintroduced to by a sheer chance of fate. She'd originally been very much in love with him but then he got a job working for the United States intelligence community. A combination of his secret job taking him all over the world, and the fact he couldn't speak about any of it made the relationship falter. My mother then met my father and fell in love with him.

Many years later, my new stepdad had been somehow contacted by my mother when looking for someone else entirely. Following that chance connection, and after a short stint at dating and getting to know each other again, the two had picked up where they'd left off. My stepdad had moved in with us after a few months of their reunification. After years of being alone, my mother had finally found her true love.

I, on the other hand, had been dealt a hard life lesson. I had to learn to live with this new guy and live under his rules. We had our issues initially, but after I had enlisted in the Marines we found a mutual respect. We weren't buddies but both loved my mom and that was common ground enough.

Since I'd been back, because of a displaced sense of shame, I had not been in touch with my mom. I felt like I was a failure since separating from the service. Not having anything good to tell her, I stayed away.

But now I wanted to tell her how well I've been doing. That was what I was attempting to do by picking up the phone. The thing was, this was only her answering machine.

'*Beep* . . .'

Our debut album *Come Find Yourself* came out in 1996 and everything changed. The single 'Scooby Snacks' became a top 20 hit in the UK and was described as 'the best song ever written about a bank robbery – and the funniest'.

As I said earlier, the spark of the idea had been the security guard called 'Mike' at Mecca, who used to have a large plastic jar filled with 10mg Valiums and ask if anyone was in need of a 'Scooby Snack'. The song Fast came up with sounded like a film soundtrack so it made sense to add in those samples from *Reservoir Dogs* and *Pulp Fiction*.

What those samples also added in was Quentin Tarantino asking for a cut of the royalties and a co-writing credit. Which kind of jaked us. But, as I said in interviews at the time, to take the samples out was like taking the paint off the painting. Once it's on, you can't do so without fucking up the painting.

The song was our calling card: as well as reaching no. 12 in the UK, it was a top 40 hit in Australia, New Zealand, the Netherlands, Ireland and Iceland, among others.

We were on our way.

'Yeah, sorry, it's me . . . Hugh.' Jesus, I never call myself that. I was just trying to tell her that I was doing ok, that's all. Breathe, kid. 'I hope you and Alan are good . . . I'm calling because I've got some good news . . .'

They were probably out doing something suburban. My mom had moved up to Cape Cod, near Boston, with my step-father a few years prior. It's a lovely part of the United States, named 'New England' because of its colonial heritage, and it has beaches and beautiful secluded areas that make it a world-famous vacation destination. I had no idea how they lived their lives anymore and realizing this made me feel sad, like I didn't even know my own family anymore. 'I know we haven't spoken in a while, but I've been working really hard on my new band.' It seemed like it was a natural thing to want to share that with your mother, but I felt like I was pleading my case to a judge instead. 'Well, we made a demo tape, like I used to record on the four-track . . .' I was felt like a 13-year-old kid trying to impress his mommy. But I *was* trying to impress her, and that was weird to realize mid-sentence. 'We did a few big shows at the club I work at, the Limelight club. That's on 20th Street and 6th Avenue; some big record industry guys saw us and signed us to an eight-record deal . . .' I didn't know how long I had before the machine cut me off so I kept it moving. 'We did it . . . I did it, Mom! I got me a record deal!'

Come Find Yourself shifted over a million copies across Europe. MTV played us on a loop, and amid the Britpop hype we became a different draw at festivals across Britain and the Continent. But our success on one side of the pond wasn't exactly matched on the other. American audiences didn't really seem to understand the package – our sound, the humour and image. That sucked. We got great reviews but not the US sales we were hoping for.

But that didn't stop us from putting a dent in the rock and roll universe. The hit singles continued. I partied alongside Madonna and Pamela Anderson, Sacha Baron Cohen and Christina Ricci. We were gifted clothes by the likes of Versace, Dolce & Gabbana and Gucci. It blew my mind that people knew who we were. At one party I was even accused of cockblocking a member of Massive Attack who was trying it on with a Spice Girl in the toilets. He was trying to poke her; I wanted to go for a pee.

'The record company, EMI, they're the ones who signed the Beatles, Mom. Crazy . . .'

I knew she'd know who the Beatles were, but the rest of it was purely my own subconscious laying it bare without considering her listening to any of it. 'I got to go into the recording studio and actually record an album . . . in a real studio like we used to talk about back in the day, Mom?'

I thought I heard something on the line. I paused and listened. Was it her? It didn't matter if she was there not answering. I was a success and if she didn't want me around anymore, just like my father didn't, fuck her too.

I had initially thought I would call up my mom and tell her not to worry about me anymore, that I was now on the road to success, but it ended up that I really wanted to tell her I wasn't weak like my father was. I wanted to tell her that despite being his son, I transcended his weakness and became the better man.

The Marines were part of me showing her I wasn't like him.

I guess a whole lot more than I would have liked to admit was to show her I wasn't like him. But it didn't seem to matter all that much to her; I was talking into a machine like a dummy. I had to wrap this up before I got cut off. I was not going to leave another message, this shit was humiliating enough. 'My phone number is ███████████ if you need it. I'm hoping to tour and if we get up to Boston I'd love it if you and Alan would come down and—'

'*Beep.*'

Chapter Twenty-Two

Lyric Writing

'Is that why you called, Huey? You felt rich, or something? Did you smell it? Jesus H. Christ, kid . . .'

My business manager Bruce was a quintessential New York music guy. He was in his mid-sixties and was always grumpy, but kind of nice at the same time.

'Bruce, I'm gonna need two business-class tickets, two connecting rooms at the Mondrian on Sunset and . . . let's say five grand in spending money, to start us off.'

'*What?!?!*' Bruce shouted down the phone.

'What do you mean "what"?' I answered, a little annoyed at his yelling at me.

There was a pause on the line and I patted Sugar on the head. I was sitting in my apartment on 8th Avenue, taking stock after an extremely long year of touring the world. I was feeling rich, but not in that sense. I felt rich because Fun Lovin' Criminals had sold over a million copies of our debut album and in doing so automatically activated the second option on our recording agreement with EMI. I was feeling rich because I was able to record a second album with my band. I was the happiest that I had ever been; I was hitting the stride I was only dreaming about just a few months before. I felt rich because I saw Joyce most every week and spoke to her on the phone when I couldn't. My girl was chill for a change and I wasn't hammering the pills and booze to sleep as bad as I had been. My life was working out.

Now, though, it was time to think about the next album. Your first album is the whole of your life up to the point you record it, the second album is your life after that, so it had better be as interesting, right? I thought that a change of scene would give me a new perspective from which I could write more stories that I could later compose into the next Fun Lovin' Criminals album. Los Angeles seemed like a place filled with stories to me: Raymond Chandler and James Ellroy painted vivid pictures in their stories about the place. It seemed a great idea to immerse myself in another city to find something new and interesting to write about the human condition. I called it a 'lyric writing expedition' and I rang Bruce to sell it that way as best I could.

Bruce, however, had news for me as well. I wasn't just feeling rich. I *was* rich, too. 'Kid, remember I just told you, you are a millionaire . . .' Bruce had answered my phone call by unceremoniously stating I had just become a millionaire.

It was quite the introduction and a useful one as he had then listened to my long laundry list of demands for my trip to LA.

'I was hoping you could book the flights through your office.' I had ignored his outburst, knowing I had this effect on Bruce most every time we spoke. 'I can come by tomorrow to grab the cash and I could pick up the tickets then . . .'

It was nice to be a millionaire, I thought to myself as Bruce did some hand-over-the-phone talking to his assistant. 'Really?' he was saying to his assistant, Cathy, who I adore by the way.

'You talkin' to me?' I managed.

'Don't start that shit with me, kid. I saw that movie at the fucking premier . . .' Bruce's firm represented half of New York's famous people, and Robert De Niro was one of them.

'I'm fucking around, Bruce, you know I love you.' I did love him, but he really broke my balls.

'No,' he continued undeterred. 'I was talking to . . . whatever. Listen, the short version is . . .' he paused for dramatic effect '. . . remember I just told you you were a millionaire? Kid . . . you're not a millionaire anymore.' Bruce took my silence for some kind of shock. It wasn't, I just wanted the tickets booked before I lost the seats. I was waiting for Bruce to calm down a little bit, but he raged on: 'Looking at the flights and that Mondrian hotel . . . shit . . . how much a night?'

'Yeah, Mondrian,' I answered curtly, still a little annoyed.

'Yeah, kid. Not even bringing in the five K spending money you want . . .' he got solemn '. . . you just dipped below being a millionaire by about 30 grand or so. But knowing you that'll double by Thursday . . .'

Easy come, easy go. Even by my standards, being a millionaire for a matter of minutes was fast work.

'Was he the bass player?' asked Mateo.

'Nah, his name was Brad. He's the drummer.'

My man Mateo was negotiating the traffic on Mulholland Drive in our rented Land Rover Discovery. I was rolling a doobie on the rental agreement in my lap as Mateo and I made our way down the hill into Hollywood. Life was good.

We'd just left our friend JK's crib, where we'd met Brad Wilk, the drummer from Rage Against the Machine. In his youth JK had nicknamed Flea from Red Hot Chili Peppers. Now he sold weed to make ends meet. We'd been there, like Brad, to grab some Hindu Kush he'd just harvested. Brad was a really cool guy and despite Mateo's confusion was most definitely the drummer. He and I both worried JK was gonna get caught by the cops. He was drying his very stinky weed in his backyard surrounded by a tiny bamboo forest. It smelled something crazy all over his block and it seemed just a matter of time before the police came calling.

Out in the Hollywood Hills with Mateo and the big Land Rover, Bruce and his bullshit back home seemed a world away. We were jamming DJ Z-Trip on Power 106 and the sky was heading towards a beautiful southern California purple sunset. I zoned out to the music and scenery out of my window.

The mood was only tempered when Z-Trip finished abruptly. Left without any theme music to continue our quest, Mateo was now looking for tunes, scanning the FM dial. I lit a joint and passed it to him while I took over the search. I got us to some soul station that was just ending a news segment: '. . . and now for some baby making music . . .' the DJ purred, and Barry White started up. 'Let the Music Play'. Mateo and I nodded at each other: we both instantly knew this was the station we should be listening to.

'Barry White!' Mateo exclaimed.

'Yeah, Barry White,' I countered.

'Barry White . . .' Mateo parried.

I said the first thing that came into my head. 'Saved my life . . .' I continued, back in time with the music.

'Barry White?' Mateo was genuinely interested.

'*He got you back with your ex-wife . . .*' I sang.

'Barry White?' Mateo asked, all curious.

'Barry White,' I answered conclusively. I pointed to the side of the road and Mateo steered the big SUV over. He turned to me as he pulled up: 'Was that . . .?' he paused.

But I finished up for him. 'Yeah . . . it was.'

It was epic. We had just written a song. I took a pen

from my backpack in the backseat and wrote the words 'Barry White Saved My Life And Got You Back With Your Ex-wife' on the back of the Hertz rental agreement. I laughed out loud. Mateo joined in. After a while, we got a hold of ourselves.

'That's one done ...' Mateo said as he signalled into traffic.

'Sure is, bro.' I looked at my watch and saw we were going to be a little late meeting our man Sal. But given we'd just written a song, I reckoned he'd forgive us.

Sal was Sal Jenco, who alongside Johnny Depp owned the Viper Room nightclub on the Sunset Strip. Ever since Fun Lovin' Criminals had played a gig there the year before, we'd become good pals with him and Johnny. Sal had very kindly offered to show Mateo and myself around while we were in town, and tonight we were meeting him at the club before it opened.

Buoyant from our Barry White revelations we pulled up into the lot of the Viper Room and parked the big SUV by the back of the club. Sal was stood by the back door talking to a woman with blonde hair. As I came up to him he waved hello. 'Huey! How you doin'?' Sal said in his best 'back home' voice.

'I'm good, my brother,' I laughed. 'Just got back from JK's house over the hill.' I looked over at his companion.

I immediately recognized her. It was a very newly famous beautiful blonde movie actress.

She smiled and said, 'Oh, this is Huey?'

I took this moment to deflect. 'Yes, I am him,' I tried to remain calm and enunciate. 'Aren't you that famous actress . . .?'

Sal cut into my soliloquy. 'Yeah, Huey, she is . . .' He made a face like I just got off the boat, or plane, in my case. 'She and I go way back, right, kid?'

The lovely actress giggled the same way she did in the movies. 'Yes, Sal is my . . . pal.'

At this point Mateo ambled up too and I made the introductions. She continued to be really cool with the pair of us. At one point I paused the conversation to ask if it was ok to smoke the joint I had rolled earlier. Everyone agreed – it was Hollywood, after all.

'My boyfriend is from New York,' she admitted between puffs.

I clocked Mateo's disappointment as she passed him the joint. Like he had a chance. 'Really?' I asked her. 'Where in New York?'

'New Rochelle, I think.'

'Oh, yeah. That's just above the city, in Westchester County.'

She nodded and took the doobie from Mateo, who was doing a great job of not showing how excited he was to be smoking a joint with a famous Hollywood actress.

'His parents ... still ... live ... there.' She coughed violently between words.

She was one cool woman. After a few more passes of the joint she bid us all farewell and drove off into the night in a small dark green sports car.

Sal gave me a look like I should recognize his demigod status and laughed. 'Bro, what kind of shit was that?' He tried to mimic my mannerisms but it just made him, ironically, look like a cooler version of himself. 'Aren't you that movie star? Duh!'

I laughed along with him and Mateo and told them the truth. 'That was what I thought at the time ... Shit, Sally, she is that actress.' I continued to point out the obvious to further hysterics.

'Yeah, but ... Hey, that reminds me.' Sal scratched his head to get the thought fully out of it. 'The girls told me that they took you to the Tenacious D gig last night. When you entered the club, Jack stopped the show and broke your balls? Really?'

'Ah, yeah.' Last night was starting to come back to me now. 'It was crazy.'

When we arrived in Los Angeles Sal had assigned two of his friends to 'look after' us while we were in town. His friends were two wild LA chicks: they didn't have to tell us they were exotic dancers when Sal didn't have them chaperoning us around, but they did anyway.

'Mateo and I had just killed a few chili dogs at Pink's when the girls called telling us about the Tenacious D show,' I started to explain.

Mateo laughed out loud at the mention of Pink's: it's a hotdog stand on North La Brea Avenue in Hollywood that makes the best chili dog on earth. People always talk about In-N-Out Burger, but Pink's is the real LA spot for me.

'When we opened up the curtain to go into the club, from the lobby . . .' I outstretched my arms '. . . Bam!'

'Yeah, bam!' Mateo echoed my sentiment.

'So there we were,' I continued, 'all four of us and . . . Jack?'

Sal nodded at me with the same look he'd given me about the Hollywood actress. 'Yeah, Jack Black. Another huge star . . .' He rolled his eyes at Mateo.

'Shit, I don't know anybody . . .' I said defensively. I don't, I can't really remember people's names from TV or movies – been that way my whole life. 'Anyway, Whosiwhatsit stops the fucking song and goes, "Hey, the gig started at ten." And then he gets the crowd to boo us.' Sal is almost doubling over at my retelling. I was not so amused. 'Your boy Jack is fuckin' crazy. What a voice, and the other guy . . .'

'Kyle,' Mateo came to my rescue.

'Kyle, yeah. They're great, man. The gig was so much fun.'

'The band broke up mid-set,' Mateo added. 'Jack went

over to the far side of the stage and started talking shit about Kyle . . .'

'Yeah, that's part of the show,' Sal explained. 'But the ball breaking was improvisation, I'm sure.'

Sal was a super good guy and even though the two chicks he selected to be our tour guides were scandalous strippers, Mateo and I were having the time of our lives out here in Los Angeles, California. Which reminded me. 'You hungry, Sally baby?' I asked after we'd finished with the joint and the ball breaking.

'Why, where you thinking of going?' Sal rubbed his stomach.

Mateo and I looked at each other and replied at the same time. 'Pink's.'

Chapter Twenty-Three

Latham Road Trip

'It's not that bad, baby . . .'

She was looking like I had just told her I was never coming back, or something. Her brown eyes showing a bunch of emotions all at once. We were in Astoria Park by my apartment in Queens and it was just after five in the morning. I had just gotten back from the studio in Manhattan and now I was trying to explain myself to her, stoned as fuck. 'I'll be gone about four weeks.' I was holding her head in my hands, trying to show her that this separation was going to be difficult for me as well. 'I'm gonna miss you every day, girl.'

She wasn't buying it, I could tell. She moved her head to the side and walked away leaving me alone on the path.

I called after her, 'Hey, you can't be mad at me for following my dreams . . .'

She had stopped at the sound of my voice.

'I've got to do this and you know it.'

She turned to me and wagged her tail.

'I've got a great place for you to stay while I'm away.'

The tail stopped abruptly.

I'm pretty sure Sugar knew more words than she let on. 'Bath', 'vet' and 'out' were ones she openly admitted to understanding. But 'away' was a new one for me to see her react to.

Sugar and I were as close as a dog and a person could be. When we ate, we ate together; she slept in the bed with me and, on top of all of that, this dog was privy to many of my darkest secrets. We had spent all of our time together since we began our partnership, and now that I was having to travel and tour with Fun Lovin' Criminals I had to make sure someone was looking after my dear dog.

'You remember Tim from the studio?' I asked, like a mom trying to convince a kid of some such nonsense. 'The redhead dude who had a dog with the same name as you . . .?'

Tim Latham, our esteemed engineer and new friend, had told me about his dog growing up and how her name was Sugar too. He also told me his dad, a recent widower who was also a retired New York City police lieutenant, was open to the idea of dog-sitting Sugar while I was on tour with U2. Tim's little sister still lived at home as well, and she was psyched to have a dog in the house for a month or so. Since Tim's mother had passed away they hadn't had a pet in the house, and everyone thought it would be a nice change of pace.

Sugar was tilting her head to the side as I described Tim to her again. 'About up to here . . .' I put my hand up to my brow to estimate Tim's height. 'Crew-cut, looks like a cop, acts like a cop.' Shit, it must run in the family. 'Anyway, his dad is cool as the day is long and he's down to look after you at his place out on Long Island.'

I always spoke to Sugar like she was a person – it was just how it was. When I had a problem or couldn't sleep, Sugar listened to me. When I was having a nightmare or a mental health episode, she was there for me, wagging her tail being an angel with fur. I loved this dog for real, and the idea of her being on Long Island chilling at my man Tim's father's crib getting all the good treatment, made me feel less devastated about leaving her behind. 'Tim has a little sister . . . and she loves dogs too.' I was trying to convince myself as much as I was Sugar, but she seemed to get what I was saying. Sugar was walking alongside me now, nose up smelling the approaching dawn.

The sky was brightening behind the Manhattan skyline just over the river. The park was right on the East River where it met the Hudson River at the Triborough Bridge and it had amazing views of the Manhattan skyline. It was a clear day dawning and that seemed appropriate. I had thought a whole lot lately about how I was now at the dawn of a new chapter in my life. So far it was everything I had hoped it would be up to this point: the record deal was very well negotiated and we were enjoying some early success with our debut album.

Even so, I was still fighting my inner demons on a daily basis. I had become used to taking a pill to sleep and another pill to calm down when I got too stressed because the trauma I was suppressing was not being addressed. Joyce had become a huge help in my life, and I endeavored to see her about once a week. Seeing her regularly kept me focused on my mental health journey. But I still relied on the drugs and booze to get me to sleep. I needed that focus with everything else popping off.

I kept most of the really tough times to myself. I always told Joyce how I was feeling after the fact. As much as I trusted her and spoke to her frankly about how I felt, there was a sense of loneliness in me that compelled me to do the hard stuff on my own. I guess my mother had tipped me over the edge when she took off with my stepfather and left me to figure most of my life out by myself. I have a serious self-reliant streak that manages to weave itself through most of my life, and when I decided to ask Joyce for her help I had to make some decisive changes in how I operated.

One of the staples in my daily practice to get my mind right was to go outside as much as I could. Walking Sugar around was how I did this. Heading off on tour, I didn't know how I would manage not having my two or sometimes three daily walks with my furry chum.

Seeing that I was deep in thought and missing the moment, Sugar bumped her head against my leg to get my attention. As I looked down to her she gave me a tail wag and made me feel like I was the most important person in the world.

I hadn't made a connection this deep with my girlfriend Belisa, who was on again off again. Belisa believed I wasn't making enough progress in the endeavour of me turning into someone she thought I should become. I had a few vague ideas of who I might want to be but they weren't lining up with hers and that pissed her off. I didn't want to be around someone who was pissed off I wasn't someone else, so we didn't hang too much anymore.

As Sugar brought me back to the moment and reminded me of the approaching dawn I continued to reassure both of us with empty platitudes. 'I think they'll spoil the shit out of you, girl . . .' I stopped and bent down to grab her furry face again. 'And when I get home I'll get us a huge pepperoni pizza from the spot near our old haunt back in Brooklyn . . .'

I felt close to tears, which wasn't great. Crying like a baby in Astoria Park at five in the morning was potentially physically dangerous.

What was I going to do without my dog? I was already a

mess, and knowing that I was going to be separated from my closest friend filled me with a sadness I hadn't felt for a very long time. I had lost a few friends in the Marines, and this was in that ballpark as far as my physical reaction. I was literally feeling sick and couldn't think past the point of Sugar and me parting ways.

The one silver lining was the fact that Tim Latham was a man of great character. He kept his word and was, deep down – and past all the macho bravado we all play around with – a kind and decent man. That doesn't happen by accident, and I deduced this was because of his upbringing. If his dad was in charge of my dog, I was satisfied with the dude, for sure. I told Sugar all of my concerns, and she rolled her brown eyes like I was overreacting. Maybe I was, maybe I didn't know if I could make all this happen, and just maybe I was using my severe case of separation anxiety as cover. However I sliced it, Sugar was going to be just fine. It was me I wasn't too sure about.

The U2 tour was big time. I hadn't played a show bigger than a few thousand before, and that crowd was by accident. Could I do it? Could I actually do this big fucking football stadium tour with U2?

It looked like any concerns I had needed to be hashed out before the inevitable day arrived like an overdue train. Was there some kind of book I could read to teach me how to entertain multitudes? In the past, if I had thought that I didn't fully understand something I wanted to I would read five or six books to get a better understanding of the subject from many different points of view. But, alas, there wasn't much at Barnes and Noble and nothing at the Strand on Broadway about huge-scale musical entertainment for beginners.

The book that I did find a whole bunch of things in that helped me form a plan was Carlos Castaneda's *A Separate Reality*. That old book was one of my 'original ten' books that I kept with me through my time in service. Its dog-eared pages were littered with my margin scrawl from years gone by. In that book I found a way to remove myself from the equation.

Sugar was my whole world at that point. All of my friends had their separate relationships with her, and even my girl-friend knew that it wasn't going to be a good move to try to come between us. I hadn't thought about how much I spoke to her until that morning, and once I had, I was completely embarrassed.

As we got up towards the deli by the north side of the park the sun had crept up on us without me noticing. I looked back to see Sugar wagging her tail at me, still thinking I was the most important thing in the world. The sun's sharp angle caught me lacking and I tried to blink it away. Sugar thought I was crying again and, up on her hind legs, came in for a hug.

'Hey, kiddo, are we cool with all this?' I asked her smiling face full of teeth.

Her tail told the tale.

'Ok, then, let's get a few bacon, egg and cheese ...' The tail stopped. She'd heard a word she knew very well. 'I know, girl, one for me and one for you.' The tail resumed its wag and I left her outside to talk to Eddie the Bum who was singing some Greek song softly to a tree by the curb. It smelled like spring today and I took that as a good omen. I was indeed in the spring of my life. Hopefully growing out of who I was into the man I needed to be was the trajectory this tour would point me on.

I got three bacon, egg and cheeses from Yannis at the counter and tossed Eddie the Bum his as I came back outside. Sugar and I crossed the street and picked a bench to have our last breakfast together on for a few months. She sat next to me like a person and leaned against me.

That broke my heart a little.

Chapter Twenty-Four

Road Trip to U2

I heard the tour bus before I saw it. It made its way down 18th Street and 8th Avenue with an expensive rumble and a satisfying '*psst*' as it hit the brakes. I glanced out of my window and gulped at the size of the silver-and-black Prevost in all its sleek glory. My ride had arrived and then some. I couldn't wait to get on it and leave my troubles behind.

The band were going out on tour with U2 as the opening act for part of the US leg of their PopMart tour. Our debut album had been out about a year and we were getting some commercial success in Europe and Asia already. Then the guys in U2 asked for us by name to do these shows in America with them. We'd not yet cracked the States so got busy saying yes.

The USA is huge when it comes to music. Rather than there being one massive market, there are hundreds of local markets that you have to spend a bunch of money and a whole year doing the rounds to hit individually. That was what every new band had to do to get over in America. Rather than starting from the bottom up, we now had an opportunity to do it in style with one of the biggest rock bands in the world.

As we prepared to do these dates with U2, I got into a big argument with my now live-in girlfriend Belisa. When I told Mike Schnapp about my domestic disturbances he suggested I hitch a ride with him and our soundman Kirk on the tour bus. The first gig was in St Louis, Missouri, and the bus was meeting Mike and Kirk in Manhattan before heading west the next day. It felt too good an opportunity to turn down.

I had bought a four-foot-long glass bong on St Mark's to commemorate the event and keep me and Mike occupied on our journey. Mike approved wholeheartedly while Kirk, who didn't smoke, stayed up front and mostly kept to himself. Mike showed me how to make use of the back lounge's ice cooler hidden in a side table by the window. He revealed that you could gain a higher 'high' by using ice in the bong to cool the smoke and increase your ability to inhale. This was the inspiration of what Mike called 'Huey's Meet and Greet with America'.

We would sit in the back lounge of this amazing brand-new tour bus with the window wide open smoking the four-foot-long glass bong. It was too big to smoke by yourself, so we had to be together just to get the bong lit. As we would rumble on down the road with the breeze blowing in, I would wave happily to the passing cars and trucks. People would slow down to peek in the window with the billows of blue smoke emerging like a brush fire, only to be met by me, an unknown, smiling and waving like a mental patient.

A key player in this adventure was George Hampton, our tour bus driver. George was a US Navy vet from Vietnam and a real gentleman. He reminded me of a character from the book *Confederacy of Dunces*. Not at all to say George was a dunce – to the contrary, he was one of those Southern men from a bygone era portrayed beautifully within that book's pages. I knew a few men like him in the Marines; they were quick with a laugh or a shotgun, your choice.

George and I bonded on the first night we drove into the interior of America. We talked a little about our service, and how he was in the shit in Vietnam. The 'Nam vets I've met have a calmness when they're around us young guys, and I took that as a sign that even though things for me at the time were hard to deal with, if you didn't cash out and kill yourself, you could actually lead a good life free of the visible signs of trauma.

George was proof of that. There was lots going on inside him, but that was his personal struggle. Us veterans who are fighting a silent war inside can endure a whole lot more than we think we can, when we know we're not burdening our people. Family and friends can understand only so much, and this is how similar men who've served in the military, regardless of different ages, bond.

'Son – it's ok I call you "son"?' George asked that first night, with me sitting next to him in the front of the bus in the jump-seat.

'Sure, George, it seems like a thing you'd do anyway,' I joked.

'Well, ok, son . . .' he smiled. 'I ain't gettin' you drunk and then pissin' you off . . .' George had all these pithy sayings that I wish I could remember more of to put into my country songs.

We smoked his Chesterfield cigarettes until the sky started to brighten and talked about stuff I don't care to share about his time overseas but, suffice it all to say, this man was the real deal, and I have great affection for him. He liked me too, and he loved Mike.

We had made an arrangement that night that whenever we were approaching a big Walmart store or a barbecue joint of some renown, George would buzz us on the intercom on the bus and he would tell us how far to go until stated destination.

On the drive west we stopped at a Walmart in Paradise, Indiana. I was trying to buy a pellet gun when George saw me and came over. 'Say, son, you want me to buy you a real one?' he stage-whispered to me. 'I got me a federal permit.' He patted his hip where his S&W .45 ACP was holstered. 'I roll coast to coast, with the help of Smith & Wesson – and the Holy Ghost . . .' He was a master of this frontier gibberish, and I ate it up. It was a kind offer, but I knew that a firearm in my illegal possession would not add to the rock and roll adventure I was on.

'Oh, no, George, it's cool.' I stammered a little because Mike, who was not a gun guy at all, was standing next to me holding a huge three-foot round Frisbee. The Frisbee had all these weird hippie colours that melted into each other. It looked like Mike was very fond of it by the way he held it up like a shield. 'Don't shoot!' Mike shouted jokingly at George.

George put his hands up in mock surrender but you could see in his eyes, this was for real. He really wanted to know if I needed a heater.

'Hey, it's cool . . .' I caught his smiling kind eyes. 'I'm happy with this vermin-vanisher.' I held up the cheap Daisy air pistol in its box. It looked like an Olympic target gun with an optic sight and a moulded wooden grip.

'Ok, son . . .' George finished. We both had a giggle because we both knew I was right, but I knew the offer still stood by the handshake he gave me.

'Those hot wings are world famous, son. Go on, grab you one of those 'fore that redhead steals your wallet . . .'

I looked over my shoulder and in the dim light I could see her through the smoke. We were sitting in a strip club in a strip mall on an industrial park across the street from a chemical plant. To top it all off, it was ten in the morning.

'Shit, George, she's staring at me and everything, damn . . .' I looked sheepishly back at my wings and dipped one in the blue cheese dressing. I don't like ranch that much. The wings were quite excellent but I was a little bleary from sitting in this joint all night waiting for George to get his 'straight eight'. By federal law a bus driver has to take an eight-hour break after driving for a certain amount of time. So while George was resting on the tour bus, Mike and I had chilled for a bit in this joint waiting for him to wake up and come get us. By the time George had appeared in the strip club, Mike had disappeared off into the VIP room. George reminded me I had a huge gig that evening across the Mississippi River at Arrowhead Stadium. The rest of the band and crew had flown in the previous night from New York.

'Y'all can get some shut-eye before the soundcheck.' George was looking at his vintage Rolex Submariner watch he'd bought in some Post Exchange in Europe on his way to Vietnam for two-hundred dollars. 'Y'all's got rooms in the five-star hotel where U2 are staying, the Ritz-Carlton.'

George's face was caught in the strobe of the flashing lights from the stage where the redhead was eyeing us up. He turned serious. 'It's a big deal you guys playing these shows with them Irish boys,' he continued. 'Son, Mike told me that the record company has invested a whole lot of money and time into you boys.' He winked at me. 'You, Huey, are the star that all these other cats are going to be casting their dreams onto. I've seen a whole lot in my life and one thing comes to mind here . . .' He lit a Chesterfield and winked at a waitress passing our table before continuing. 'Nothing forced is ever beautiful, son.' George nodded to himself like he just realized how fucking profound he'd just been. I was sobering up to his advice and nodded along. 'This new life of yours will ask a whole lot of you,' he explained. 'You sure know what duty is, but don't confuse that feeling with doing things you know are too much.'

I was really appreciating this early morning pep talk and told George as much. 'I always wanted this, man,' I made an open-armed gesture encompassing this scene before us both, laughing.

'It's better than the infantry, son. But I'm as serious as a priest in a paddy wagon.' George leaned in. 'These folks will expect a whole lot for their investment, and you, young corporal, have to understand how much you can give before it takes too much and leaves you for dead by the side of the road like a one-legged rabid possum on a cold rainy night.'

This was something that I needed to hear. I was meeting up with the boys later at the hotel before we all did a soundcheck at the stadium and was feeling a little apprehensive about these shows we were about to play. I still hadn't really thought about what I would do to entertain tens of thousands of people. I figured it was going to be like playing for hundreds of people but scaled up for size and sound. I knew how to entertain, but I was still learning a whole lot about that every day.

This gig with U2 would be like getting a university degree in being an MC. A master of ceremonies, or MC in hip-hop terms is someone who leads the proceedings and controls the levels of crowd participation. Traditionally, my role fronting Fun Lovin' Criminals meant being the MC, telling my stories along with a guitar. I also sang a little here and there to carry the hook of the song. I was hoping to add some miles to that ethos, to road test it and make it better.

My work ethic regarding my musical development was based on how I achieved things in the Marines – through sheer strength of will and violence of action. I brought that intensity and focus to being the front man of FLC, but I knew deep down that no one was going to help me carry the band in the way I had help in the Corps. I was literally on my own with the conceptual stuff and overall vision concerning the band's sound and image; it was, after all, my band.

I couldn't let myself fail. I would be letting too many

people down. That realization could force me to give away too much of myself personally, and that was what George was talking about. *You, young corporal, have to understand how much you can give before it takes too much and leaves you for dead by the side of the road.*

'Don't let them make you see yourself as a worker.' George was getting his shit together on the table in front of me. His tiny cell phone and huge ring of keys were sitting next to his two empty cans of Dr Pepper. 'You're an artist, don't forget that, my boy!' As he was picking his bits and pieces up, Mike returned from the VIP room, smiling.

'Hello, my good friends!' Mike was sitting down as George got to his feet opposite. Mike saw George rise and said, 'Did I interrupt anything . . . serious?'

'Not a chance, Miguel.' George always changed Mike's Anglo name to a Spanish one for shits and giggles. 'I was just telling our young friend here how much is riding on him.' George gave me another wink and said to Mike, 'Just a few warriors planning an attack.'

'Yeah, and like the man says,' I chimed in, 'I'm happy the whole situation is relying on me, because I'm the only one I can trust.'

'My man,' Mike agreed. 'If it wasn't for you we'd all be in trouble.'

'Shit, this ain't trouble, right, buddy? Wink-wink, motherfucker . . .' George turned towards the door of the club. We watched as he sauntered down the bar, tipping his imaginary hat to the inert dancers along the way.

I turned to Mike, 'Living legend, bro . . .'

'Fuckin' A, Huey,' Mike replied. 'Fuckin' A.'

Chapter Twenty-Five

All the Time in the World

Later, when I got back home, I told Joyce about the tour and how well we did. I also told her about what George Hampton had told me and how I was now thinking a little more about the people around me.

I had gone through a trial by fire doing those shows. Shit, I had to walk out onto a stage in front of over fifty thousand people every night, who did not want to hear from me, and in the span of a few minutes get them onside. I had no way of knowing how to do this. There wasn't some YouTube video explaining how to work a massive crowd 'like a pro' in five easy lessons. I'm not sure there even was YouTube back then.

I didn't know any famous musicians to ask them how they pulled it off, so I had to wing it, a process that came at a high personal cost. In order to internalize my stress and not show the people around me I was struggling, I had a prescription thing happening from my old shrink, and booze helped kick all that in. It was a shitty Band-Aid but it was all I could do to keep it together.

I dealt with the situation by changing my conscious focus from my personal perception to another perspective. I got the idea from the meditation I was trying to do every day in a new bid to be more in touch with myself. By removing myself from the thought process that freaked me out – being onstage without a clue as to how to entertain – I thought instead about what it would be like to be a fan in the crowd. What would I want to see and hear from the opening act at a huge U2 show? This process allowed me to make a hasty plan of attack: nothing fancy, just a few initial moves. Like a good chess player, I would adapt to the changing environment, anticipate and then improvise. Just like a hip-hop Thelonious Monk, battling my demons live, but not making a big deal out of it.

I thought to myself about all the songs we were playing and how much information a normal person in a huge crowd could take in if they weren't really paying attention. I then formed the plan of attack.

First Move. Let everyone know who we are and who we are. That's not a typo, but the way I reminded myself to be clear about mentioning the band name as much as I could. If you liked what you heard, I deduced, you would make a short effort to pay closer attention, and you might become a fan.

So at that time, and at as many other times as I could arrange during our short 45-minute set, I told everyone clearly that we were Fun Lovin' Criminals and we were from New York City.

The move worked. Before long Mike Schnapp and I would wander the arena's parking lot at the gigs all around the country, and a few in Canada, looking for the live-news trucks with the dish on top and we would bag ourselves live on-air interviews from just the word-of-mouth from previous shows on the PopMart tour. The name was getting out there and it was great to see that happen after all the hard work and internal struggle.

Back to the war plan . . .

Second Move. Tell them how happy you are to be playing for them in their superior town to the last town we played, and thank U2 for asking us to perform for their lovely fans . . . But remember to not get in the way of the First Move.

For the moves to work, authenticity was crucial. I could do all these 'moves', but if I was being inauthentic, it was all for nothing. People can see through bullshit, they do it every day in their lives; the last place they want or deserve to get some fake-ass bullshit is in their dose of popular music, thank you very much.

Every night before we hit the huge stage opening up for U2, I would bring a cocktail shaker and some fixings up to the wings, which were actually below the stage, and make a couple of tequila shots for the boys in the band and our crew.

The first night of the tour, we were all kinds of nervous. There were about sixty thousand U2 fans we had to entertain, and the first round went down too easy. As I was making round two U2's stage manager came up to see if we were about ready to go on. 'You boys opening up a pub?' he asked, his very official radio headset dangling carelessly from a hip holster like a gun-slinger.

'Kinda . . .' I offered him a plastic cup as he came into our little circle.

He took the cup and smiled to the band and our crew guys. 'I'm Gerald, the stage manager, we met before at soundcheck.' We all nodded, shook hands and then I poured out the shots to the attending degenerates.

'Grab your cup if you know what's up!' I shouted to my congregation, the first shot having already warmed up our collective disposition. I looked around to my bandmates, Fast and Steve, and our crew . . . and Gerald. 'To Bess Truman!' I exclaimed.

'May she rot in hell!' replied my band of crazies, loudly . . . as Gerald almost spat his shot out. He managed to swallow the concoction and pulled a pleasant face.

'Very nice, Huey. What's in it?'

Fast jumped in lighting his cigarette off the butt of another.

'We call it "the Fun Lovin' Criminal". It's got tequila . . .' He looked over to me laughing.

'A whole lot of tequila,' I nodded at Fast.

He continued, smoking furiously, 'And Rose's lime juice, that's important . . .' He searched for the word. 'It's a "cordial", not straight nasty lime juice . . .'

We all pulled a sour face at the straight lime juice line, and he took it onboard and continued speaking to Gerald, who I was pouring another shot for.

'. . . And then it's a tablespoon of sugar, to give it that "last sip of the Margarita" feeling.'

Gerald downed his second shot. 'Boys,' he nodded, 'if you play half as good as you talk shit and make drinks, this is gonna be one helluva tour.' With that he looked at his watch and let us know we had five minutes to show-time.

The next night Gerald asked if it was cool if he invited a guy named Dallas, who was The Edge's guitar tech, along for our pre-show drinks. We all hung out before the next show and talked about Edge's massive guitar rig and drank tequila.

The following night The Edge himself appeared with Dallas and Gerald and a few of the Belgian riggers who built the massive set every night.

The set for the PopMart tour was considered a crazy stunt by a lot of industry folks. The huge TV screen was the world's largest, and the surrounding speaker fixed smack dang in the middle of this huge McDonald's-style yellow arch was set in, of all things, mono. The whole show wasn't some state-of-the-art 'six-way stereo magic' set-up, it was everything down the middle, as we say in the studio. It made for a well-balanced sound for the punters: you didn't really get a bad spot in the whole arena.

The head engineer, Joe, made it backstage for a few shots later in the tour and told me how crazy it was to, 'Fly this huge fucking "areoplane" into the clouds every night with these mad Irishmen . . .' We hit it off famously, and during the tour I spied Edge and Bono watching us from peep holes cut into the set of the stage at various points, beaming like proud uncles. That was a little intimidating, but what was I going to do? Fold like a chair because some famous guys were watching me do my thing? Not likely.

Four nights in and The Edge brought Bono himself to our little drinks soirée and he had a grand time with us, so much so we went on ten minutes late. Gerald wasn't about to tell Bono to hurry up and finish his story just to keep to a schedule.

The evening after that Larry Mullen and Adam Clayton showed up, who are both absolutely lovely men. We would refer to U2 from then on as our 'rich uncles'. They are still very rich and still considered family.

When we heard we were going to open up for U2 at the Meadowlands, we went crazy!

The Meadowlands is an outdoor sports arena complex in New Jersey that is synonymous with New York and American Football: the New York Jets and the New York Giants both use the complex as their home stadium.

But there's also another story in the history of New York that Meadowlands is famous for. Back in the 1970s, Jimmy Hoffa, the labour union leader and longstanding President of the International Brotherhood of Teamsters (IBT), disappeared. As well as being a union boss, Hoffa reportedly had links to organised crime. The urban legend goes that Jimmy was clipped by the outfit and his body was dumped in the concrete that was poured into the foundations when the Meadowlands was built. The times kind of match up and it's still a mystery as to what actually happened to Jimmy, so when we played two nights at the Meadowlands opening up for U2, we made the best of it.

Up to that point we had been rocking our 45-minute set, making our cool music sound great and making good connections with the crowd. We'd blaze, get some drinks and watch U2. After a few nights on tour we had thought we were doing really well, the management of U2 – Paul McGuinness and his team – were friendly and giving us very positive feedback and our crew were being told by U2's crew that we were smashing it.

There was no time to try to process all the stage moments, there had been so many times I'd caught me and my guys really killing a particular song, or getting a crazy response from the huge crowds, but I always took a moment too centre myself before going onstage.

These moments of reflection took place in the porta-loo that was placed at the bottom of the stage, just for us musicians. I would compose myself after our tequila shots and think how some or all the members of U2 took a piss here. I gained perspective in there, I remembered that 'this too shall pass', and maybe the next porta-loo I took stock of myself in would be something as insane as this one.

At one point in our first show in New Jersey, about halfway through our set, right before I played, 'King of New York', I spoke to the crowd of 70,000 like we were cousins, which we kind of were. 'This is an incredible night, thank you everyone!' Can I get a "hell yeah"?' I asked my thousands of new best friends.

'HELL YEAH!' most of them roared back, which fortified me for my next bit.

'Some of you may have heard of a guy named Jimmy Hoffa . . .' I paused to let my voice carry all the way to the back of the football stadium and when I heard my own echo return and a rather large murmur from the assembled multitude, I continued with my observation. '. . . Well, if you know the legend, he was buried here where they poured the concrete back in the day.'

I paused again but this time it was for comedic effect.

'Shout out to my Teamster brothers and sisters . . .' I added, my tongue firmly in my cheek.

Another rather large groan of laughter mixed with cheers for the union crew egged me on further. I was doing a stand-up routine and the locals were eating it all up, thankfully.

'It was supposed that he was poured into one of the end zones. So it seems, my new friends . . .' I waved my hands at the crowd in an exaggerated greeting. This slight pause was met with huge cheers, it was our hometown gig, and there was a big group of FLC fans in the crowd, and apparently a whole bunch of new ones by the response.

I kept my pseudo-preacher New York schtick going full blast and, mixing my American sport analogies, hit the home run, no pun intended. '. . . It would seem that a band called Fun Lovin' Criminals and seventy thousand of y'all are dancing on his grave!' I smiled my biggest shit-eating grin and gave Fast the nod. Fast nodded back and made eye contact with Steve. Fast hit the sequencer and the click track lit up Steve's in-ear headphones, which he wore to hear all the sequences we used live and also the other instruments. Steve then gave me a 'one-two-three-four' and then started to keep time on his hi-hat while I played the intro guitar part.

Man, I could get used to this.

*

After one show at Camp Randall Stadium in Madison, Wisconsin, U2 asked me, Fast and Steve to be their guests on their private plane back to Chicago where the next three shows were taking place. The plane wasn't some small private jet, but was a big old girl they named *Air Lemon*.

Air Lemon was set up to hold a bunch of people in the back in really nice first-class seats. Up front, past a few spacious bedrooms and a massive galley, the U2 guys had their private area. Bono and Edge were really kind and generous with their time that evening and asked me to hang with them up in this private area for take-off.

When we had gotten our pre-flight drinks from the stewardess and were getting settled, a man who looked like he might be one of the pilots came up to Bono and Edge, seated near each other by the front bulkhead. 'Good evening, Bono.' A nod to Bono was returned with the expected panache. And then another. 'The Edge . . .' Edge nodded back appreciatively. Bono did get most of the attention so it was good to see my man Edge getting some flowers. 'Whenever you say . . .' This pilot wasn't wearing a formal jacket depicting his rank but his ease around the 'client' and his solid gold 1970s Rolex GMT, along with his epaulettes' four gold stripes, all pointed to him being the captain.

'Huey, you all set?' Edge asked me.

I smiled like I had been caught stealing. 'Sure am,' I saluted with my Black Label on the rocks.

Edge turned back to the captain and replied to his question, 'Indeed, Randy, we are . . .'

And with this command relayed, the captain left us and I heard a door close beyond the bulkhead. After a few seconds the huge airplane began to creep into the fading light of the late Wisconsin summer.

Holy shit!, I thought to myself. These guys were shaking my whole fucking sense of reality here. This was real freedom. They had a plane that left when they wanted. The rock and roll dream was alive and thriving. I had never seen this type of thing up close and personal before. It was intoxicating to be around, and I maybe got a little too heavy a dose that night.

When the plane paused on the taxiway aligning itself with the runway, I motioned to Bono with my joint in my hand as if to ask permission to light it up. We had been smoking cheeky cigarettes away from public consumption for a few minutes already, so it wasn't like I was causing a ruckus.

Bono nodded with a chuckle. He did that a lot around me, laughing at my 'youthful exuberance'. He once told me it was because of what I did next.

As *Air Lemon* started her taxi and began to pick up speed I stood up and grabbed the two seat-backs on either side of me. As I stood in the aisle, joint firmly lit in my mouth, smoking out this small private seating area, the plane started its 'rotation' and began to leave the ground. Never had I ever dreamed I would at any time in my life be doing this kind of shit, ever. I was revelling in the moment and holding on a lot harder than was actually necessary, when I turned to see Edge and Bono smiling at me like I was . . . well, a fucking psycho.

'What?' I asked, trying not to drop ash all over the carpet.

Bono took my cue. 'You seem to be enjoying the plane ride, my boy . . .' He was patting the seat next to his. 'Let's have a sit down and enjoy the flight.'

I sat down and gave Bono a big old hug.

'Uncle Paul' – I had begun to call him that after he said 'Uncle Bono' sounded fishy – 'you guys are chilling like the Caesars of Rome could only have dreamed of!'

At that revelation, Edge gave us a good old guffaw and we smiled like we had it all.

It was true, though. These cats were no small-time operation. This was rock and roll on the highest level. I was getting to experience this anomaly in the space-time continuum, up close, learning from the last of a dying breed: the real rock stars.

The money they were working with rivalled some nations' GDPs, but they had the dexterity to keep the ball moving in any direction the four band members and their esteemed and very cool manager Paul McGuinness decided to go at a moment's notice. This was demonstrated by our departure from Wisconsin. As we were chasing the sunset west towards Chicago the guys were telling me what they were planning for the next few days.

Bono told us about this party thing they did when the tour had a few days in one town and the crew didn't have to break down the set after the show. The band threw the crew a party in the arena somewhere free of charge and called it after an Irish pub, but personalized to fit the occasion, 'The Riggers' Arms'. The riggers who built the stage were mostly from Belgium and they were all highly trained technicians. They also loved to drink, which endeared them to the Irish like you wouldn't believe. U2 even sent *Air Lemon* on a round trip to Ireland and back to pick up fresh kegs of Irish Guinness especially for this event. It was before all that global warming carbon footprint shit.

'You guys should do a private gig for the crew!' Bono was excited for a few days without the travel and always enjoyed a party.

'Hell, yes! We will, Uncle Paul!'

And we did, but we put a little twist on it.

Instead of performing as Fun Lovin' Criminals, we called ourselves 'Mysterious Ways' and played punk rock covers of U2 songs, with a few of our own to break it up. It was a lot of fun and it all went great. On the second night Bono came up onstage with me and sang a duet of 'We Have All the Time in the World'. It was one of those moments you never forget. As the song goes, '. . . *nothing more, nothing less* . . .'

Acknowledgements

In the writing of this book, I have been blessed working with people who have made a great effort to allow me to write this story just as I wanted.

These people are Rory Scarfe, thank you for being a mensch and my agent, in that order.

Tom Bromley, thank you for helping me form a plan and then making that plan into a book.

Richard Milner at Quercus, thank you for your enthusiasm and guidance in uncharted territory.

Additional shouts to my kids, Beaumont and Indiana; I love you very much, but may this book be a deterrent to you doing as much dumb shit as I did.

I would like to also acknowledge the friendship of Mateo, Joyce, King, and Mike Schnapp.

Lastly, to all of you who can't see past your pain, have hope and stay strong; this too shall pass.

Semper Fidelis, HM